# OVERCOMING THE BENCH

A Baseball Guide to Players, Coaches & Parents

## BOBBY BROWN

**Bobby Brown Baseball Co**

Overcome the Bench

www.bobbybrownbaseballco.com

Special Thank You To:

My Wife Stefanie

My Parents Bruce & Kellie

My Coaches Sam Blalock & Andy Lopez

My Frozen Ropes Coach Curt Holcombe

My Arizona Baseball Teammates

My Grandparents & In-Laws

My Daughter Joelle

Overcoming the Bench

A Baseball Guide to Players, Coaches & Parentss

Bobby Brown

ISBN (Print Edition): 978-1-09831-828-4

ISBN (eBook Edition): 978-1-09831-829-1

# Table of Contents

# Foreword

I dedicate this foreword to Bruce, Bobby, Bradley and Britts. Thank you for giving me, "The time of my life."

My son asked me to write the foreword for his book. Where do you start? I could start when he was 4 years old and I took him to the park and we were playing catch. I beaned him right in the nose and he said he never wanted to play baseball again. Ironically, what he said a few months later while we were watching a Padre game in San Diego, he said, "I will be there someday." I thought nothing of it until….14 years later.

I would tell parents that have a child with a special talent to get ready for a wild ride. I'm not talking about a child that does well at something. I'm talking about a child that you already know that he/she is a "freak." You will spend more money than you have to help them achieve whatever that greatness will be. You will refinance your house, put 350 thousand miles on your SUV so you can hang on to the journey. There is nothing to prepare you for this. Starting at the age of 11 or earlier, every other weekend you will be in some other town for a tournament while your child balances little league and school. If you are good enough you will be asked to play on a pro Scout team. We did that for 2 years during the week and on weekends. Bobby doing his homework in the car for the 2 hour ride each way from San Diego to LA and back was common.

And if that is not enough, he played International baseball for 2 summers. If your child ever gets the opportunity to play International ball, do it. You meet players, parents and coaches from all over the world. Even though we mostly could not communicate, we did so with baseball. The pin trading and jersey trades were so much fun. I actually think the parents enjoyed the pin trading more than the kids. The jerseys that we have from other countries are priceless.

If your child is a "freak," you will have coaches fight over your child. There is the potential for the parents to be jealous. Don't be a part of their drama. This is why we always sat beyond the outfield fence and almost never in the stands. It likely fueled them, but we did not want to be a part of that. We were fortunate to be a part of this team that had no such drama and jealousy when Bobby was around 12. With this team we played a tournament in Colorado with 64 teams and we placed 9th. We only had 9 players for this particular tournament. No one could get hurt and everyone had to pitch. Pretty amazing and I have to say it was really fun to run rule the other teams by the 4th inning.

Don't forget about those hitting instructors to tweak this or that to prevent the, dare say it, 'slump.' I tried never to mention the 'S' word. Too much pressure. I felt my role was to keep everything organized, supportive and be the 'safe island' in the middle of this madness. Be aware some head coaches will try to change your kids swing causing contradictory information to the hitting instructors' philosophy.

We figured that Bobby played around 1,500 games before he set off on his journey at the University of Arizona.

My thoughts on college are this, if you're lucky to get a scholarship it likely won't be much. Do not expect a big one. There are only 11.7 scholarships available for each DI Team. So do the math. 35 players and 11.7 scholarships. If you can get an academic scholarship to help great, but do not count on this. When Bobby's team went to the College World Series and won, we financially could not attend. Just not a dime left in the coffers. Watching on TV from home was not the same, but still an amazing thing to see your kid hit a home run in the Series and become," 1st Team All-Tournament DH."

You will have many ups and downs. Anyone that knows baseball at all knows that there is lot of failure. Try not to ever get to high or too low. It's impossible though. After a rough tournament or game, my husband would go over and over and over what went wrong. Blah

blah blah....Sometimes it was just too much and I would cry. Then I would think to myself, why am I getting so upset over a game? There is no crying in baseball.....right?

One thing I know is that quite a number of coaches and scouts get hooked on some kid and that kid gets drafted. Many of those kids are generally oozing with talent, but lazy. I guess they are hoping for the so called "upside." The whole thing is really just a big guess. And boy do they get it wrong when they get it wrong. It seems that some do not do their homework on a kid. When you are around baseball all the time you know all the players. Some kids have a ton of talent but are miserable to be around. Bad attitudes can ruin a team. Try not to get too pissed off about this. Life is not fair. Bobby did not get drafted, but you will read in this book that Bobby did have the opportunity and was signed as a free agent by the Kansas City Royals. The key is just having the opportunity.

The journey is more than just baseball. It teaches the players and their parents about life. Make this a family journey. I always tried to have our other 2 children feel special too and all the traveling together makes for so many family memories. The long drives, double headers in 120-degree heat, the spectacular wins, making sandwiches at 80 MPH in the car and the family time at the hotels is priceless. We turned many of the trips into mini vacations, sightseeing; and visiting family along the way. Who doesn't want to see the world's biggest thermometer, pan for gold, visit the oldest water tower in some city or play I Spy in the desert?

I am thankful for Bruce's (Bobby's father) extensive knowledge about baseball. Having played the game through college and semi pro, he was able to navigate, 'the ropes' of the game where I could not. When it's all over you will miss it terribly and realize through all the ups and downs you were really having the time of your life.

# Introduction

The dugout can be the loneliest place on a baseball field. You are so close to the action but when you don't start it is easy to feel far away. I played college baseball at the University of Arizona for five years with most of it in the dugout. It was not until my fifth and final year that I became an everyday starter and finally showed once and for all what I was capable of doing. Those who would have walked in my shoes would have quit the game but I am not that kind of person. My options were either to have patience or to quit. I was told by many that I needed to leave Arizona and go play somewhere else. I might have been somewhat crazy for staying but the success of my final year showed why patience was the right path to follow. There were times where I thought quitting was the right path but my heart kept pulling me back telling me this is my year to shine. A blind person could see that I was talented with the tools to play professional baseball. In order for me to play professional baseball there were a few things I had to accomplish. First, I had to take advantage of my opportunities, and second was to become an everyday starter. After spending so much time on the bench, I couldn't wait for those opportunities to come. 2012 was my final opportunity to get off the bench and achieve my dream. Before I get into 2012, I need to back up to when I was a kid.

I have been fortunate enough to be blessed with a natural baseball ability, which has allowed me to hit a .300 average and sometimes much better every year growing up. Baseball has always been my life, and I can't remember a weekend where I was not doing some sort of baseball activity. I played in many tournaments as a kid, and have had at least a few thousand at bats leading up to college. It is safe to say that baseball was more important to me than anything else. It seemed like everyone I knew had known that I played baseball and that I wanted to be a professional player one day. The only thing I talked about was baseball. When someone would ask how my weekend was, I would mention something baseball related. It is hard to imagine how different my life would be right now, if I had never played or had given it up at an early age. I couldn't give it up because I was so good at it. Like most boys I played little league as a child but as I got older, I played more competitive baseball and joined travel teams. I was fortunate to take numerous lessons and have the support of my family growing up. My family spent a significant amount of money on me in support of my dream of playing professionally.

I went to Rancho Bernardo High School in San Diego from 2003–2007 and played my junior and senior season on my varsity baseball team. My high school baseball program has always been considered elite. My Head Coach, Sam Blalock, is the winningest high school baseball coach in San Diego history. The well-known baseball book *Moneyball* by Michael Lewis, which even turned into a blockbuster hit starring Brad Pitt, mentions my high school baseball program calling it, "The Factory." Billy Bean, the man behind the book *Moneyball* and General Manager (GM) of the Oakland Athletics played for Sam Blalock when he coached at Mt. Carmel High School in San Diego. Numerous players had gone on to play professionally and/or had gone to a Division 1 college out of Rancho Bernardo under Sam Blalock, and I wanted to keep that tradition going. Notable players are Cole Hamels, Trevor Williams, and Hank Blalock. After a solid junior season hitting .400, I knew I needed to start thinking about the future and find a college program that will take my talent to a higher level. I received numerous letters from college baseball programs who were interested in me. After visiting a few schools and participating in their camps, there was one school that stood out the most. In the summer of 2006 I went to a baseball camp at the University of Arizona. After performing well, I was the Most Valuable Player (MVP) of the camp and soon was eager to commit there. Little would I realize this experience would be the start of a long career at Arizona spanning from the fall of 2007 to the spring of 2012.

It is amazing how the decisions you make in your life affect your future. I think about it all the time, "What would my life be like if I had gone to another school?" I received hundreds of letters from different school telling me they were interested. I believe that everything happens for a reason. If I had not gone to the University of Arizona, I never would have won a National Championship, and I never would have met my future wife. All my hard work would eventually pay off when I signed my professional contract with the Kansas City Royals. Despite my roller coaster experience as a student athlete, everything that I went through was well worth it. Sometimes it is better to not bounce around from school to school, and stick out a commitment. When my time was up in 2012, I walked away with a National Championship ring, the girl, and a professional contract. Though I am not playing anymore, I am fortunate enough to be giving back my knowledge of the game by coaching. I hope that my tips on how to play this game the right way, and my story of perseverance and commitment can help aspiring ball players achieve their dream of playing professionally one day.

# 1

# Freshman Year

I came out of high school with a chip on my shoulder and a high degree of confidence. I figured that the vast success I had accomplished as well as coming from a top Southern California High School, Rancho Bernardo, had prepared me for the next level. I have always been that kind of guy that can join a team and make a profound impact to the point where I turned into the number 3 hitter in the line-up. Essentially, I have always been "the guy" on every team I have played on. There has never been such a humbling baseball experience in my life than that when I went to college. In all honesty I didn't recognize the fact that the Pac 10 (Pac 12 now) was such a competitive and difficult league before I joined college. I immediately noticed that everyone was bigger and stronger than me. For the first time in my baseball life I was overwhelmed. The 2008 team was full of All-American sophomores and juniors who were on their way to getting drafted. We were even pre-season # 1 in the nation in 2008.

## Fall 2007

The fall of 2007 was a major shock to my system. I came to Arizona as a first baseman, and that's where I figured I would potentially see myself playing in the future, especially when our big power hitting senior first baseman would be leaving the next year for sure. Scrimmage games were my chance to prove to the team and coaches that I belonged there. What amazed me the most was the pitching. Just about all the pitchers on the team threw in the 90's and at least three threw over 95 mph. The bullpen talent was off the charts. Ryan Perry and Daniel Schlereth, who eventually went on to pitch in the Majors Leagues with the Tigers were hard throwing pitchers with incredible off-speed pitches. Our closer, Jason Stofull, who went on to play in the Minor Leagues was virtually impossible to hit. Our ace pitcher, Preston Guilmet, who pitched briefly in the Big Leagues, was a work horse and made college hitters look silly. I simply could not hit against these guys. Every strikeout was like a hammer nailing my confidence into the ground. I was almost afraid at the plate, to the point that I would be out before I even stepped into the batter's box. I am not sure of the exact stats but I recall going at least 3 for 30 during our Fall intra-squads. After a less than stellar fall I was told that I would have to red-shirt my freshman year meaning that I will not be playing at all this year.

## Benched

When the season began, I did not know what to think for I had never spent a significant amount of time on the bench. While I was once "the guy," I was now on a team with a bunch of "guys." There were 45 players on the roster and many were in the same boat as me. Not being in the dugout cheering on my team was a new experience for me and the only way I recall feeling was uncomfortable. During our PAC 10 home games those that did not play sat in the stands and watched the game in street clothes. We did not take part in any of the pre-game warm-ups either. It was not required for us to go to the games and I remember not going to some of them out of disgust because I didn't feel like I was part of the team having to watch from the stands. Those that redshirted and didn't play also did not go on the road trips leaving us with a lot of free time. I chose to make the most of my free time by hitting in the cages and weight lifting so I could always be fresh. As difficult as it was not being in the games, I sucked it up and thought in the back of my head that next year I will get my chance. My team was dominating every team we faced like everyone expected. We cruised into the playoffs defeating Michigan at their regional. By this time school was over and I along with those that did not play were sent home. On TV I watched my team's dominance come to an end when we lost to Miami at their super regional while being one win from going to Omaha. Omaha is the home of the College World Series. Going to Omaha was always the goal of the season, and now that it did not happen, I hoped one day I could experience it.

# 2

# Redshirt Freshman Year

After redshirting my freshman year, I returned for my second year with a sense of confidence that I would finally get a chance to play. After a solid Fall in our intra-squad games, I expected to finally play. However, that was not that case for I got 5 at bats the whole year. I got 1 hit in those 5 at bats on a 2009 ball club that was full of selfish and immature individuals. The team had talented players but many of those individuals could care less about how the team did. The whole year I observed this from the dugout and expected my opportunity to come based on the lack of team success. Our last regular season series was at Oregon but mathematically we were already out of playoff contention. Therefore, we were playing for pride. During the trip home we were told from Coach Lopez that we were going to have a team meeting when we get back. We got back to our locker room around 11:00 p.m. and had a two-hour meeting that lasted till 1:00 a.m. The meeting was well-deserved. While some guys sat there about to fall asleep from the long day, I remember sitting there angry that I didn't play the whole year and felt like I wasted my time at Arizona. Needless to say, I saw no future for me at Arizona, so when I had my individual meeting the next day, I mustered enough courage and told Coach Lopez that if I wanted to have a career in baseball I need to leave and go somewhere else. There was no plan to cut me and, I was told by Coach Lopez that I should have played more. Despite this, my decision was final and I now needed to look for a new school.

## A New Beginning

When I got home, I thought through my best options before I went off a week later to Virginia to play summer baseball. I decided the best path for me was to go to a local community college near my home and possibly get drafted or transfer to another Division 1 school after one year. However, two weeks after joining, I told the Community College Coach I would not be attending anymore. This is why: I received a very unexpected phone call from my Assistant Coach at Arizona. He explained to me that they had made a lot of changes, cutting a majority of the team, and that he wants me to return because he felt I had a future in the program. I had already made the tough decision of not returning to Arizona, and now I had to make another tough decision whether to come back or not. This was a stressful time in my life; when I received the call, I was in Virginia playing in a summer league. After long discussions with my parents, we came up with decision to come back to Arizona essentially believing this would be a fresh start. My summer in Virginia was amazing, I ended up hitting around .350. I even made the all-star team and got MVP of the game. That summer revitalized me mentally and I planned on bringing that confidence with me for a fresh start at Arizona on a new team.

# 3

# Redshirt Sophomore Year

My third year at Arizona felt like a fresh start. It was the first time in three years that I felt like I was part of the team. I made the transition from first-base to the outfield by myself because that was the only place I knew I could start defensively. I had a solid fall and felt confident that I would see a ton of playing time. Many starting positions were open and it was freshmen who were going to fill them. There were five freshman who stood out as great players, namely, SS Alex Mejia, Starting pitcher Kurt Heyer, 3B Seth Mejias-Brean, and outfielders Joey Rickard and Robert Refsnyder. All of these players went on to play professionally, four of which made it to the big leagues. You could tell these guys were really gifted and we could win with these guys. When the season began, I was the opening day starter in left field. However, in my first two at bats I did not get a hit, so the coaches decided to take me out and put Robert Refsnyder in instead of me. In his first at bat he got a hit and needless to say I was pissed off. I wasn't mad at Robert because he didn't do anything wrong, I was mad for having such a small opportunity. My role thereafter was a pinch hitter role for the following couple of weeks. I got some at bats here and there and did well. Then things began to go my way. While injuries are never a good thing, it does open up opportunities for others. Our starting second baseman and first baseman got hurt and couldn't play for most of the year. Because of this I split time at left field and designated hitter (DH) the whole year. I did not play on a consistent basis as much as I should have but I got 133 at bats and collected 39 hits, 12 of which were doubles. We made the playoffs and went to the Texas Christian University (TCU) Regional that year. We defeated Baylor in our first game but lost to TCU the following day to put us in the loser's bracket. The next day we lost to Baylor and had to go home. What upset me the most was I was not given even one at bat while we were there, after helping the team get to the playoffs. I love to compete in a high-pressure situation. I was ready to get after it and help get us to Omaha but I never got the chance. The next question that comes up is – Why would I stay for another year? What stopped me from leaving was the belief that my playing time can only build up from here. I was about to go into a very important season such that if I did well, I could get drafted. At this point I had been there for 3 years and invested so much time into not only the baseball program but in academics as well that leaving all of it would have felt like I wasted my time.

## Politics of Baseball

This was the season where I really learned about the politics of baseball. I learned that if you were not on scholarship, you really have to slug the ball on a consistent basis to be in the line-up. I was not on any scholarship money, which I believe significantly influenced the lack of playing time I had received in 3 years. Those that were on scholarship got most of the opportunities. Many times, I would scratch my head asking why this person is getting so much playing time. I believed the answer was scholarship money, which makes since. Every year I would ask my Assistant Coach for scholarship money and every time I continued to get a 'no' from him. I at least deserved to get money to handle paying for my textbooks. I had busted my butt on the field and worked hard to get good grades but he did not acknowledge this. As the three years had gone by with no scholarship, I needed to start getting student loans. The cost of tuition seemed to rise every year and this not only took a toll on my family but it also affected families of many other players as well. Not to say my decision to go to Arizona was a mistake, it was not, but my advice to those wanting to play college athletics is to seek out an athletic scholarship, and hopefully you can get an academic one as well.

# 4

# Redshirt Junior Year

Based on the success that I had in 2010, I felt very confident going into the season. I looked at the positives of the previous year and not the negatives. I had proven to the coaches that I could play in the PAC. My once slim 170-pound body was now at 200. I was even one of the fastest runners on the team. 2011 however was a different story. Like the previous year I started the first game in left field. I went hitless the first game, which led to future big leaguer, Johnny Field, getting an opportunity to play over me. In his first collegiate at bat he hit a home run. After that occurred, I just knew that I was in for a long season personally. Johnny ran away with his opportunity leaving me in the dust. My mentality was in the drain and I had flashes of the 2009 season in my head with the amount of playing time I had. However, I was older now and I knew feeling sorry for myself would not make me feel better. I knew that I would get more opportunities at some point. The tough part was waiting for them to come. When they did come, I did take advantage of them. However, my little successes did nothing for me to earn a spot in the line-up. Again, I was not on any scholarship. While I figured I had to at least get some at bats in the DH spot, the line-up was consistent and didn't change. The starting first and second baseman who were hurt last year were now healthy and were everyday starters.

## 4/5/11 vs. Arizona State

During particular points in my career I felt compelled to document how I felt after certain games. During the 2011 season I recorded two separate games which illustrate my time on the bench to how I succeeded off of it.

I sat through yet another game watching my team be embarrassed again from our rival. Offensively it was tough to see the momentum of the game on our side and then a couple poor at bats ruined the inning. I sat back and watched while thinking that I should be hitting in this situation. Like always, I imagine myself in that situation and pulling through, and feeling that amazing feeling of driving in runs. From experience, getting that key hit is the best feeling in the world, especially in a big game. Early in this game, about the 4th inning we had high energy where we almost got into a brawl because their pitcher kept hitting us. The benches ended up clearing but we did not fight. The only person who got thrown out was our ineligible bullpen catcher who came running down all fired up screaming f-bombs while spitting tobacco on the umpire's arm when they were trying to stop him. After all this we failed to maintain the momentum when our junior left-handed pitcher who throws 95 mph failed to throw strikes and walked half the Arizona State team. His poor pitching in turn affected our defense. From then on, our hitters just looked silly and couldn't put an inning together. After the game, our Assistant Coach gave us an hour-long talk. He pointed out one of our key players who is likely going to be a high draft pick and told him he has the worst approach at the plate, is unaggressive, and is screwing us right now. Then he said, "Guys like Bobby Brown have been waiting all year to play and would gladly be in your place." Here I thought to myself, "Maybe you should let me take their place." When the meeting was over, I went home in upset from having gone through a long meeting.

# 4/8/11 vs. Cal

We played a great game against Cal. In the 8th inning my Assistant Coach told me I was for sure going to hit. I was going to hit for my teammate who struck out three times already and looked horrible. So, when the inning started, we were losing 2-1. We got some players on base and it was now time for me to go on deck to hit for my teammate. We ended up scoring while I was on deck. Then as I walked to the batter's box my Assistant Coach told me to go back and have my teammate, who I was replacing come back. I awkwardly walked back to the dugout and his at bat resulted in a pop out on the first pitch in the infield. I was pissed because there were runners on first and second and it was a great opportunity to give us the lead. We failed to get any more runs after the pop out. The score remained tied 2-2. In the top of the 9th Cal rallied to score 2 runs making the score 4-2. My anger rose because I felt that if they had just had faith in me to get a big hit in the previous inning, the situation we are in now might be different. So, the bottom of the 9th came and my Assistant Coach tells me if the first batter gets out, then I am hitting. The first batter did get out and I was able to get an at bat. Filled with anger for the lack of faith in me from earlier I went up to the plate. On a 2-2 count I drove a double to the left center gap. From there the next guy walked. Now with runners on first and second, the next batter hit a chopper over the third baseman giving him a double that scored me and my teammate who was on first base to tie the game. Now with the game tied 4-4 and a runner on second our catcher came up and delivered a walk-off single. We all went crazy with excitement as we rushed the field. The credit for the win was given to me for starting the rally. For me it was a greater feeling when everyone was pushing me with excitement than it was to get the actual hit. I proved to everyone like I always have that I can succeed in a tough situation.

Just when I finally started hitting the ball well and got some playing time after my double against Cal, I broke and dislocated my left index finger in practice. This occurred towards the end of our regular season in early May. When I saw the x-ray, I couldn't help but to let out tears. I had surgery the next day and I have to give credit to my doctor for doing a great job. I ended up having a small plate and 4 pins in my finger to fix the break. The doctor informed me that if I have some aggressive rehab over the next couple weeks, then I could be swinging the bat soon. Just for the sake of it I snuck down to our batting cage and wanted to see if I could just swing the bat the day after my surgery even though I wasn't supposed to. I was able to do so by gripping the bat with nine fingers but obviously it was awkward. The rehab was painful but I just prayed that it would allow me to be back with the team and I would somehow get a shot to play. My shot did come on 5/28/11 against Washington, around 2 weeks after surgery. I pinched hit and was able to drive a single between the first and second basemen. At that time, we were tied 5-5 in the 9th inning. After a ground out that got me to second base and an intentional walk to the next batter, one of my teammates delivered a walk off hit that drove me in. The team swarmed me in excitement and it was a rewarding feeling. What made the moment a little sweeter was that the doctor who fixed my finger attended the game, obviously hoping that I would enter the game. He was ecstatic to say the least and I gave him a hug after the game and thanked him for doing such a great job. I started the next game, which actually was our last regular season game. I did not get a hit but I drove the ball hard all over the field, just right at people. I was satisfied because I was back in action. For the playoffs we were sent back to the state of Texas for the Texas A&M regional.

## Texas A&M Regional
## June 3rd, 2011 (Arizona 0, Seton Hall 4)

First game of the Texas A&M Regional can be described as a fail. We came into the game heavy favorites and our confidence was very high. The game started at 12:35 p.m. and it was 100 degrees with high humidity. I did not start. Kurt Heyer, our ace, started the game, and was a little shaky; leaving balls up in the zone. For the most part he did a good job getting himself out of jams. However, in the 4th inning there was a total melt down defensively. Seton Hall scored 4 runs. When we got in the dugout our short stop called out our catcher for a poor throw that led to 2 runs for the other team. An argument ensued and it was clear that we had lost all poise. Offensively we simply could not hit or get anything going when we did get a hit. A total embarrassment to say the least. We lost by the final score of 4-0. Now we have to win 4 straight games to move on to a Super Regional.

## June 4th, 2011 (Arizona 13, Wright State 0)

I remember clearly Wright State did not want to be there after we started scoring a few runs early. It was another hot game but we were ready to play. Our offense did a great job of driving in runs. This led me to get one at bat in the 9th inning in which I grounded out to second base. Now we have to win a double header tomorrow to stay alive.

## June 5th, 2011 First Game
## (Arizona 6, Seton Hall 0)

Pretty much the same atmosphere as the previous game. Seton Hall just looked tired and look defeated once we started scoring runs. We did not score a ton of runs but one was all we really needed. I did not play. Now for the night game against Texas A&M we must win.

## June 5th, 2011 Second Game
## (Arizona 7, Texas A&M 4)

The atmosphere of the game was crazy. There were at least 4,000 people there and they were loud for the whole game. Josh Garcia shut them up in the 2nd inning when he hit a home run. Tyler Hale started for us but in the 3rd inning he took a line shot off his throwing elbow, which later we discovered was fractured. As a result, Nick Cunningham had to come in. He looked very comfortable and confident on the mound despite not pitching for a long time. I ended up replacing Josh in the 6th inning as the DH. There was a runner on second with no outs and my job was to pull the ball to move the runner over. I hit a hard chopper to second base, and ran it out for a hit. In the 9th inning Matt Chaffee pitched and somehow, he could not find the strike zone. The crowed got really loud, stomping on the ground and chanting Matt's name to mess with his head. He walked three batters and balked three times, and they scored twice. It was a crazy and stressful inning but Matt got the job done. Now we play tomorrow and the winner goes to a super-regional.

## June 6th, 2011 (Rained out)

We were completely ready to go but a few minutes before we were going to start, lightning and rain showed up. We should have just played a day game instead of a night game. Now we play tomorrow.

## June 7th, 2011 (Arizona 0, Texas A&M 3)

So today was the big game with lots at stake. Because of the day off we started with Kurt Heyer since he had another day of rest. He pitched his butt off, only allowing 3 hits through seven innings. Unfortunately, we could not score any runs; we out hit them but could not score. Our best opportunity was when Jett Bandy was on third base and Alex Mejia hit a flare to center field that dropped in; Jett was only about three feet off the base and ran as soon as the ball hit the ground resulting in him being thrown out at home plate. I did not start the game but was going to hit for Jett in the 9th inning. I was 4th up in the inning but the first three batters got out. We lost disappointingly 3-0. We had a charter plane that was scheduled to either be going to Tallahassee, Florida or back to Tucson. We went back to Tucson. We said 'bye' to our seniors and went home disappointed. Today was also day two of the draft and 5 players from our team got drafted. I talked to a Royals scout who had been contacting me when I was back in Tucson. We spoke on the phone and I told him I was ready for the opportunity and I am completely ready to go to the next level. I did not get drafted though but there is the chance of tomorrow.

## June 8th, 2011

I did not get drafted; I was glued to the computer. I was not surprised for I had only got a measly 33 at bats this year, a significant decrease from the previous season, and not enough playing time to get drafted.

# 5

# Redshirt Senior Year

## Statistics leading into 5th and final year

| Year | AVG | GP | GS | AB | R | H | 2B | 3B | HR | RBI | TB | SL% | BB | HBP | SO | OB% | SB | ATT |
|------|-----|----|----|----|----|----|----|----|----|-----|----|------|----|-----|----|------|----|-----|
| 2009 | 0.200 | 7 | 0 | 5 | 0 | 1 | 0 | 0 | 0 | 1 | 1 | 0.200 | 1 | 0 | 1 | 0.333 | 0 | 0 |
| 2010 | 0.294 | 46 | 33 | 126 | 18 | 37 | 12 | 3 | 0 | 17 | 55 | 0.437 | 14 | 1 | 25 | 0.366 | 6 | 9 |
| 2011 | 0.333 | 17 | 7 | 33 | 6 | 11 | 2 | 1 | 0 | 5 | 15 | 0.455 | 2 | 0 | 8 | 0.361 | 0 | 0 |
| Total | 0.299 | 70 | 40 | 164 | 24 | 49 | 14 | 4 | 0 | 23 | 71 | 0.433 | 17 | 1 | 34 | 0.364 | 6 | 9 |

My 5th and final year was finally here. Good changes were happening.
We got a new Assistant Coach who I connected with, we moved into a
new baseball facility down the road from our old one called Hi Corbett
Field, and I received a partial scholarship. With this new facility it gave
us the opportunity to potentially host a regional and super regional. It
was once a spring training facility for the Colorado Rockies but now
was all ours. During the fall we practiced at our old field while Hi
Corbett was getting worked on. What us players immediately noticed
out of Hi Corbett was the large size of the field. Our Head Coach saw
this size of the field as an advantage because it forced us to not swing
for the fences, but rather line drives in the gap. The five freshmen from
the 2010 season were now juniors and with me ready to lead the team.
After the disappointment of not making it past a regional the last two
years we were on a mission to Omaha.

I came into the year hitting a career .299. I began the year as the DH and stayed there most of the season. Oddly enough it took a long time for my bat to wake up. I started the year 4 for 27 and it took me my first 15 at bats to get a hit. What made things more difficult was that I briefly lost my DH job to a freshman. He came in for me on fire and it seemed he would be staying there for a while. There were 15 games that I did not start. The lack of success and loss of my starting job pissed me off but motivated me to keep working. I was embarrassed and angry, but I have been here for a long time. I know that opportunities will present themselves at some point. Over the course of sitting out I knew I had to work harder both physically and mentally. Our Head Coach always talks about being ready because you never know when your chance will come. I increased my focus during practice and hit extra in the batting cages when practice ended. All of a sudden, things started clicking for me and I took advantage of those opportunities when they finally came. I earned my way back into the line-up and I made myself some lasting memories for the rest of the season.

UA outfielder Bobby Brown has recovered nicely from an early season slump. After starting the season 0-for-14, he now has the team's second-highest slugging percentage.

# Brown coming on strong

*Senior outfielder is becoming a key part of the UA's lineup despite a slow start that got him benched*

By Kyle Johnson
Daily Wildcat

On 24 March 2012 at Oregon State I finally hit my first collegiate home run, and it was a big one. We were tied in the 9th inning at the score of 3-3 and I led off the inning. The count was 2 balls and 2 strikes and I got a fastball down the middle and pulled it to right center. My immediate thought was that it would be a double but somehow it just carried and hit off the top off the fence and went over. I didn't know it went over the fence; I just put my head down and ran. I finally learned it was gone when I looked at the umpire standing by second base who was wiggling his finger in the sky signaling it was a home run. What made the moment so great was that it had given us the lead in the 9th inning and the chance to win it in the bottom of the 9th inning. Amazingly enough our freshman catcher Riley Moore hit a home run right after me. The back to back home runs caused Oregon States fans to finally be silent who were rowdy the whole game. We won 5-4.

Arizona senior outfielder Bobby Brown slides into third base during the Wildcats' 11-7 win over Utah on Saturday. The UA sits in a tie with Oregon atop the Pac-12 standings after it has won each of four conference series it's played, two of which were on the road.

On 30 March 2012, we played against number 2 nationally ranked Stanford. We had anticipated this game all week, facing a great team and their Friday night ace Mark Appel. Our stadium was packed full of fans and the energy was electric. It was a tough game, both Appel and Heyer showed why they were Friday night pitchers. In the 9th inning we were down 7-4. However, we got a rally going and were able to close their lead to 7-5. Then it was my time at the plate. Bases were loaded and I hit a fastball right up the middle. I knew for sure the hit would tie the game but the center fielder let the ball go under his glove allowing Seth Mejias-Brean, who was on first base to score and win the game. I however was not aware of the error in center field for I had slipped and fell hard on my face just before getting to first base. When I looked up all of a sudden Seth was rounding third. I stood there like an idiot because I did not know what was happening. All my teammates were going crazy and the stadium was the loudest I had ever heard at a home game. My teammates began to chase me and I tried running away but you can't avoid a happy mob of teammates as the picture below shows. This and my home run at Oregon State rank up there as my favorite baseball memories at Arizona so far. We went on to sweep the 3-game series against Stanford.

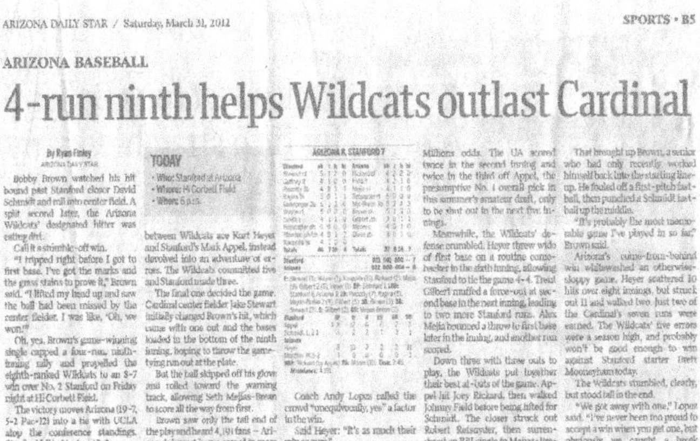

ARIZONA DAILY STAR / Saturday, March 31, 2012

SPORTS • B5

ARIZONA BASEBALL

# 4-run ninth helps Wildcats outlast Cardinal

By Ryan Finley
ARIZONA DAILY STAR

Bobby Brown watched his hit bound past Stanford closer David Schmidt and roll into center field. A split second later, the Arizona Wildcats' designated hitter was eating dirt.

Call it a stumble-off win.

"I tripped right before I got to first base. I've got the marks and the grass stains to prove it," Brown said. "I lifted my head up and saw the ball had been missed by the center fielder. I was like, 'Oh, we won!'"

Oh, yes. Brown's game-winning single capped a four-run, ninth-inning rally and propelled the eighth-ranked Wildcats to an 8-7 win over No. 2 Stanford on Friday night at Hi Corbett Field.

The victory moves Arizona (19-7, 5-2 Pac-12) into a tie with UCLA atop the conference standings. Stanford fell to 16-4 and 2-2.

The game, billed as a showdown between Wildcats ace Kurt Heyer and Stanford's Mark Appel, instead devolved into an adventure of errors. The Wildcats committed five and Stanford made three.

The final one decided the game. Cardinal center fielder Jake Stewart initially charged Brown's hit, which came with one out and the bases loaded in the bottom of the ninth inning, hoping to throw the game-tying run out at the plate.

But the ball skipped off his glove and rolled toward the warning track, allowing Seth Mejias-Brean to score all the way from first.

Brown saw only the tail end of the play and heard 4,191 fans – Arizona's largest home crowd in more than four years – roar.

**TODAY**

- Who: Stanford at Arizona
- Where: Hi Corbett Field
- When: 6 p.m.

**ARIZONA 8, STANFORD 7**

[illegible]

Coach Andy Lopez called the crowd "unequivocally, yes" a factor in the win.

Said Heyer: "It's as much their win as ours."

Arizona's rally came with Mega Millions odds. The UA scored twice in the second inning and twice in the third off Appel, the presumptive No. 1 overall pick in this summer's amateur draft, only to be shut out in the next five innings.

Meanwhile, the Wildcats' defense crumbled. Heyer threw wide of first base on a routine comebacker in the sixth inning, allowing Stanford to tie the game 4-4. Trent Gilbert muffed a force-out at second base in the next inning, leading to two more Stanford runs. Alex Mejia bounced a throw to first base later in the inning, and another run scored.

Down three with three outs to play, the Wildcats put together their best at-bats of the game. Appel hit Joey Rickard, then walked Johnny Field before being lifted for Schmidt. The closer struck out Robert Refsnyder, then surrendered an RBI single to Mejias-Brean.

That brought up Brown, a senior who had only recently worked himself back into the starting lineup. He fouled off a first-pitch fastball, then punched a Schmidt fastball up the middle.

"It's probably the most memorable game I've played in so far," Brown said.

Arizona's come-from-behind win whitewashed an otherwise-sloppy game. Heyer scattered 10 hits over eight innings, but struck out 11 and walked two. Just two of the Cardinal's seven runs were earned. The Wildcats' five errors were a season high, and probably won't be good enough to win against Stanford starter Brett Mooneyham today.

The Wildcats stumbled, clearly, but stood tall in the end.

"We got away with one," Lopez said. "I've never been too proud to accept a win when you get one, but obviously we caught a break tonight."

## 27 April 2012 - 29 April 2012

We had a bye week in the PAC so we played against East Tennessee State. It is safe to say that our offense exploded. Friday, we won 24-7 and had 25 hits. As a team we had 6 triples, which was a school record, and I had two of them. In the game there were 7 total triples with one coming from the other team, and this tied a NCAA Division 1 record. I had a crazy game going 4 for 4 with 6 runs batted in (RBIs). Saturday, we won 6-4 and I hit my second home run and was 1 for 4 on the day. Sunday, we won 21-6 and again it was a hit parade. We had 27 hits and everyone contributed. I was 4 for 4 with 2 RBIs. On the weekend I was 9 for 12 with 9 RBIs, a double, 2 triples, a home run, and 6 runs scored. Because of that series I was named one of Collegiate Baseball's Louisville Slugger National Players of the week. Below are two articles written on our baseball website about me after this series.

## May 4, 2012
## By Derrick Fazendin

When most people think of the 2012 Arizona Wildcats, they'll probably remember Kurt Heyer's blazing fastball or Alex Mejia's cannon of an arm, or maybe it'll be Robert Refsnyder's big bat in the middle of one of the most potent offenses in the nation. But for 34 current Wildcat teammates, someone else will also come to mind.

"Wow man, you know it's got to be Bobby (Brown)," said Arizona right fielder Robert Refsnyder. "This guy has been through the ups and downs. If he's not one of our MVPs then I'm not sure who is."

Arizona senior outfielder Bobby Brown is currently in his fifth year with the program and represents the only true senior on the ball club. Besides head coach Andy Lopez, Brown is the only current Wildcat that knows what it feels like to experience playing in a Super Regional, as Arizona ended the 2008 campaign just one game shy of the College World Series. He also is just of two current Wildcats that are left from a disastrous 2009 season that was infamous for disappointing performances and player attitude problems.

"You know the fact that he's been here through the good times and the bad can't be overlooked," said Arizona head coach Andy Lopez." You go back to that 2009 club and he was one of the good ones for sure."

Coming into this season, Brown had never been an everyday player for Arizona. After he redshirted the 2008 season, he was mainly used off the bench during the 2009 and 2010 seasons. During the two-year span, Brown batted a modest .290 batting average, drove in 18 runs, and hadn't hit a home run in his Arizona career.

"You know it was tough to sit on the bench like that because I always knew I was a good player," said Brown. "But honestly I just tried to keep my head up and told myself I needed to work harder."

After big-time hitters Josh Garcia and Cole Frenzel were lost due to graduation and Major League Baseball (MLB) Draft, Brown finally got his long-awaited chance, as he received his first opening day start of his career this season. (**Author's Note:** This here isn't true because no one had realized this but I was the opening day starter in 2010 and 2011 but I had lost my job after the first game of the season to Robert Refysnder and Johnny Field, both future big leaguers.)

"You know I was just so excited," Brown said. "I mean, I don't think I was nervous but I was kind of like `ok I can't mess this up because this is my shot.'"

Brown went 0-3 in the 2012 season opener, and it only got worse from there. Freshman Joe Maggi soon took his spot in the starting lineup just 10 games into the season as Brown continued to scuffle with the bat.

Despite the demotion, the senior kept his head up.

"Bobby is just one of those guys," said Refsnyder. "He always leads by example. There was no pouting, he was right there with us cheering us on 100 percent."

But during his time on the bench, Brown wasn't just cheering, he was working, and working even harder than he had before.

"Baseball is a funny game, there are a lot of things that can happen with injuries and stuff," said Brown. "I was just hoping I would get one more shot."

And he did.

After losing a heartbreaking 6-5 game at Oregon State in the bottom of the 9th inning during the second weekend of PAC 12 play, the Wildcats were off to a mediocre 2-2 start in conference. And it wasn't looking any better for the 'Cats in game two as Arizona and Oregon State were locked up at 3-3 heading to the top of the 9th inning on a rainy, windy day in Corvallis, Oregon.

Then it came.

It was a moment that was more than four years in the making. Brown launched a 2-2 pitch that soared over the centerfield fence--his first career home run. Arizona would eventually go on to win the game and the series. Since then, the Wildcats have gone on to win three of their last four PAC 12 series and currently control their own destiny for the school's first conference title since 1992.

"You know we're playing really well as a team right now," said Brown. "I'm just really happy I'm contributing to help the team win."

Not only is he contributing, he's leading the charge. Brown is currently batting .345, with 35 RBI, has two homerun and leads the team with six triples in only 116 at bats.

In addition, Brown was named one of five Louisville Slugger National Players of the Week after his monster performance against East Tennessee State after he went 9-12 from the dish while knocking in 9 RBI, extending his current hit streak to seven games.

In Brown's last year at Arizona, he's doing his best to make it one to remember.

"This by far has to be my favorite I've ever been a part of," said Brown. "This is a tight-knit group of guys and I think we can make a really special run at this thing. The goal is Omaha; that's it."

## 4 May 2012 – 5 May 2012

We are back in the PAC 12 and are playing against Oregon. The craziest occurrence that happened all weekend was that on Sunday Coach Lopez got thrown out of the game when arguing a balk call. We were winning 1-0 in the top of the 7th inning when Oregon had a man on first base. Our pitcher picked him off and the first base umpire called him out. However, the home plate umpire called the pick off a balk and the Oregon base runner was allowed to advance to second base. What made this play so shocking was that the home plate umpire made the call when the first base umpire had a better view of the pitcher. Coach Lopez proceeded to walk over to the home plate umpire and he was thrown out quickly after only saying a few words. I learned after the game from Coach Lopez that he was thrown out for saying, "You have made bad calls all day." This home plate umpire is a good example as to why our society is getting softer. Coach Lopez was thrown out for calling the umpire bad, not a swear word, not calling him horrible, for calling him bad. Honestly from my perspective of the event as it occurred, the umpire was scared when Lopez approached him and with the entire crowd booing him. He wanted to end the humiliation quickly by throwing out Lopez. That next Tuesday during practice Coach Lopez informed us that the Oregon baseball players brought a bagpipe with them and played it in their dugout. What? None of us knew they had it with them nor did most of us know what it was. None of us heard them playing it or saw it. I was not sure what a bagpipe was, and what the significance of it was until Coach Lopez explained that it is meant to be played at funerals. Now why on earth would a baseball team have that in their dugout? The clear answer must be that because they won the series against us, we were now "dead." Confusing as to why a team would do this. "Bagpipe" was now our motivation to go all the way.

# Baseball reaches 2,600-win milestone in weekend sweep

*UA offense explodes for 51 combined runs in nonconference series*

By Kyle Johnson
DAILY WILDCAT

The No. 11 Arizona baseball team took the weekend off from conference play to take on East Tennessee State, and while it may have been a bye from the Pac-12, the Wildcats' bats did anything but rest as Arizona won all three games on the weekend, including a 21-6 victory on Sunday.

Arizona (29-13, 12-6 Pac-12) combined for 51 runs and 65 hits in the series, sweeping East Tennessee State (19-24) in its last non-conference series of the season.

"I was really pleased with (the offense)," Lopez said. "Pleased that they could keep that intensity and their ability to execute all weekend.

"It was obviously our best weekend offensively in a long time."

The Arizona bats came out

swinging from the start Friday and they never stopped, on the way to a season high of runs in the 24-7 victory against the Buccaneers.

Everybody just approached the plate well all weekend and stayed selfless to create runs for the team, said sophomore Johnny Field who moved over to centerfield this weekend to replace the injured Joey Rickard.

Friday starter Kurt Heyer (8-1) wasn't as sharp as usual, giving up 12 hits and six earned runs in 7.2 innings of work.

But Heyer did enough to secure Arizona's 2,600th all-time victory, making it just the eighth school to do so.

In comparison to the rest of the series, the Wildcats were nothing to write home about at the plate Saturday, but Arizona still came away with the 6-4 victory.

Starter Konner Wade (6-1) had the toughest job this weekend as the Buccaneers kept the game close, but Wade and closer Stephen Manthei were able to give the Wildcats the

GORDON BATES / DAILY WILDCAT
Arizona outfielder Bobby Brown bats against ETSU this weekend.

victory in a game where they never trailed.

Wade allowed three earned runs and eight hits in 7.1 innings before Manthei finished it off to pick up his second save of the season.

While the pitching was good, what really stood out in the game was a

solo home run that designated hitter Bobby Brown crushed over the right field wall.

Home runs have been a rarity at the cavernous Hi Corbett Field, so the long ball garnered the nickname "Downtown Bobby Brown" from Lopez after the game.

Brown said he saw the ball well all weekend and it gave him confidence at the plate — which certainly showed in the box score. The redshirt senior went 9-for-12 on the weekend with 9 RBIs and 6 runs scored to go along with two triples and home run.

"I just felt great and it worked out for me," Brown said.

The Wildcat offense was back on the prowl Sunday, recording a season-high 27 hits on the day to complete the sweep over East Tennessee State with the 21-8 victory.

Every Arizona starter had at least a hit on the afternoon, and only first-time starter David Lopez finished with less than two hits in the game.

BASEBALL, 12

## 25 May 2012 – 27 May 2012

This is the last series of the regular season and we played our enemies Arizona State University (ASU). We were one game out of first place behind Oregon. Even though ASU couldn't make the playoffs we knew each game was going to be a boxing match. Due to the National Collegiate Athletic Association (NCAA) violations, ASU was out of playoff contention so they had nothing to lose going into this. Game 1 was a pitching duel between our Kurt Heyer and their Brady Rogers. It was a 0-0 game going into the 9th inning and Seth Mejias-Brean was able to hit a walk off double to drive in Refsnyder from second base. Game 2 came down to the last inning again. However, I came up with bases loaded, two outs, and we were down two runs. I worked the count to 3-2 against their hard throwing closer and I swung threw an off-speed pitch ending the game. I felt embarrassed and upset that I couldn't come through on this senior night. Sunday was a new day and a chance to win the PAC 12. With the game tied in the bottom of the 9th inning and two outs Jonny Field came up big and got the game winning hit. While celebrating the win we were given PAC 12 Champions shirts and put them on for the cheering crowd. To top it off, I was handed a large PAC 12 Championship trophy and I held it up while my teammates surrounded it and cheered. Oregon ended up getting shockingly swept by Oregon State, which allowed us to win the PAC 12. We did end up sharing the title with UCLA since we ended up with the same record. Nevertheless, we were PAC 12 champs and that hadn't been done since 1992. We learned during the Sunday that we were going to host a regional as well, which made this a memorable weekend.

I entered the 2012 season with just 40 starts, 164 at bats, 49 hits and 23 RBIs. In my final campaign, I finished the regular season ranked No. 10 in the PAC 12 with a .343 batting average. My slugging percentage of .560 ranked No. 5 in the conference and despite not playing in 10 games and not starting 15 I finished tied for No. 7 in the PAC 12 with 47 RBIs and tied for No. 1 with 7 triples. I started the final 32 games of the season at designated hitter with a .383 batting average, including the first four homers of my career. To top off the regular season I was honored on the All-PAC-12 team with 4 other of my teammates. I knew I was always capable of having the kind of season that I had in 2012, I simply needed that opportunity. After not playing much for four years, this was a bitter sweet accomplishment.

## 1 June 2012 – 3 June 2012, Tucson Regional # 1 Arizona, # 2 New Mexico State, # 3 Louisville, # 4 Missouri

## Game 1 against Missouri

Little can be said other than our offense simply exploded and we won 15-3. As a team we had 20 hits and I had 4 of them. Heyer looked a little nervous at first but he settled down only giving up four hits.

## Game 2 against Louisville

Again, our offense exploded for the second straight night. We won 16-4 and had 23 hits. I went 3-5 in the game with 1 RBI. We were the away team and it felt weird to be in our other dugout for the first time but obviously that didn't matter. Louisville now plays Missouri and the winner of that game will play us. Interestingly I learned that Muhammad Ali attended our game supporting Louisville since his son had attended there.

## Game 3 against Louisville

Louisville had beaten Missouri earlier in the day and now they have to play another game against us. The position Louisville is in was the same spot we were in last year against Texas A&M, so we know how fortunate we are to only have to win one game to move on. Louisville was clearly down on pitching and looked tired. Again, our offense exploded and it started with a grand slam from Johnny Field. The final score was 16-3. Field ended up getting 7 RBIs in the game. I did not contribute much going 0-5 with a walk and run scored but I am happy we won and are now moving on to the Super Regional. I went 7-15 in the series with 5 runs scored and 3 RBIs. We will be hosting St. Johns for the Super Regional and it will be on ESPN 2.

# 8 June 2012 - 9 June 2012, Tucson Super Regional

## Game 1 against Saint Johns

It was a hot game, we played at noon and it was 105 degrees. Our offense got off to a slow start and it didn't help that they scored 5 runs in the fourth. Our offenses chipped away and were able to tie it up later in the game. The game remained tied 5-5 going into the 10th innings before St. Johns scored a run to lead 6-5. In the bottom of the

10th inning Robert Refsnyder was on second base with one out, and I came to the plate. I hit a solid single up the middle tying the game. While I was on first base future big leaguer Brandon Dixon got a base hit up the middle as well and I sprinted to third base and was barely safe. Now with runners on first and third we were in a great position to win the game. The next batter was freshman Riley Moore and he walked. Now with bases loaded Trent Gilbert came to the plate with one out. With the crowd at

Hi Corbett cheering, a win was inevitable. Gilbert hit a ball in the gap and I scored easily. We won 7-6. My base hit to tie the game was a huge at bat; if I did not get that hit, we probably would have lost the game making our goal of getting to Omaha harder to accomplish.

## Game 2 against St. Johns

With the momentum of yesterday on our side we were just one win from going to Omaha. We got off to a solid early start scoring 3 runs in the first. We eventually had a 5-0 lead. Our pitcher Konner Wade had a solid game. Just when St. Johns gained momentum making the score 5-2, we pulled away in the 7th inning with a score of 7-2 after a pair of doubles from myself and Seth Mejias-Brean. In the 9th inning we knew Omaha was in our grasps. Finally, we recorded the final out and celebrated on the field. We won by a final score of 7-4. We are going to Omaha!

# 6

# College World Series 2012

**Arizona, UCLA, Florida State, Florida, Arkansas, Stony Brook, Kent State, South Carolina**
**15 June 2012 - 25 June 2012**

On Thursday we spent the day practicing on TD Ameritrade Park for 50 minutes and spent an hour signing autographs. Later we attended a banquet dinner where Nomar Garciaparra spoke to all the teams. Unfortunately, the opening ceremony set to take place in the stadium was cancelled due to a thunder storm and heavy rain. We were supposed to have sky divers and fireworks and it was disappointing to have to miss that but we hoped that the rain dies down the next day because we were set to play Florida State at 8:00 p.m.

## Game 1 against Florida State

Seeing the 22,000 people in the stands was an amazing experience. Kurt Heyer looked strong from the start and really confident on the mound. We got off to an early 2-0 start until Florida State's leadoff hitter hit a solo home run making the score 2-1. As the game went on we heard chants from the Arizona and Florida State fans, which was fun to see. We were able to get another run across the board in the 5th inning but Florida State came back to tie it in the bottom of the 6th inning. Tyler Crawford came in after Heyer and shut them down. The score remained tied until the 12th inning when Joey Rickard and Johnny Field, both future big leaguers, hit back to back doubles to finally give us the lead. In the bottom of the 12th inning with two outs and a runner on third base, our pitcher Matt Troupe struck out their hitter to end the game to give us the victory. The game felt like a boxing match where both teams exchanged blows and it was such a satisfying relief to win. I had a very poor game going 0-5 with three strike outs. It was one of those games where I swung at bad pitches and took good ones. Now we play our fellow PAC 12 foes UCLA on Sunday night.

## Game 2 against UCLA

Another large crowd on hand at TD Ameritrade Park. We had already played against UCLA earlier in the year and we came into this game knowing what they are all about. The game was simply a pitching duel between both pitchers. There was very little offense until the 5th inning when we got 5 straight hits and scored 4 runs. Myself and Seth Mejias-Brean hit a 2 RBI double in the inning. Other than that inning we could not get anything going offensively. However, that inning was all that we needed. Konner Wade shut down the UCLA offense only giving up 5 hits and did not give up a run. We won by the final score of 4-0 and this win puts us in the driver's seat because now whoever wins the Florida State/UCLA game on Tuesday has to beat us twice.

## Game 3 against Florida State

Things got off to a hot start for us; we scored 6 runs in the 1st inning. The success of the inning started with a double play ball that was hit to the Florida State pitcher and he sailed his throw over the shortstops head. From then on Florida State was forced to chip away. While they appeared to get a rally going throughout the game our pitcher Kurt Heyer got out of trouble and limited the Florida State offense to three runs in the game. The 4th inning was a memorable one for me. After walking two previous times I came to the plate with a 2-0 count and drove a fastball out to right center that sailed well over the fence for a 2-run homer. This was the second home run in the inning; Robert Refsnyder hit a solo one earlier. When I rounded first base I definitely slowed down because I wanted to enjoy the feeling for just a little longer. Now I can say I hit a home run at the College World Series, wow. We won 10-3 and now we are playing in the championship series. We await the winner of South Carolina/Arkansas game to find out who we will play.

## Championship Game 1 against South Carolina

We put the ball in Konner Wade's hand in hopes that he would repeat his brilliance that he had against UCLA. He pitched just as well throwing a complete game. In the first inning Robert Refsynder got the scoring going by hitting an opposite field two run home run. We had numerous scoring opportunities during the game and cashed in only 5 runs. In the 6th inning I pulled a single between first and second base to score Refsnyder from second base. I was 1-3 in the game with a walk and RBI. While we left many on base 5 runs was more than enough because Wade only gave up 1 run. Now we are one game away from winning the whole thing. We need to cash in more of the scoring opportunities tomorrow and have a good pitching performance out of whoever pitches.

## Game 2 against South Carolina

It was a game of little offense and domination from both pitchers, ours being James Farris. We were tied 1-1 in the top of the 9th inning; I was on first base after an intentional walk and Refsynder was on second. Brandon Dixon, who was hitless coming into the game came up with a big opportunity. He lined a ball down the left field line and scored Refsnyder to get the lead. I advanced to third and Dixon was now on second base. Trent Gilbert came up now with two outs and he drove the ball to right field scoring myself and Dixon. Now up 4-1 in the bottom of the 9th inning we were three outs from being national champs. Matt Troupe our freshman closer had the ball and things got off to a shaky start. Bases were loaded with one out after a hit and a couple walks. After a line out to second base, the last batter of the game hit a fly ball to right field and it was caught by Refsynder. We all rushed the field and dog piled on top of each other. I did my best to enjoy every last moment of the experience. What an amazing season, best feeling I've ever had. We are National Champions!!!

| Year | AVG | GP | GS | AB | R | H | 2B | 3B | HR | RBI | TB | SL% | BB | HBP | SO | OB% | SB | ATT |
|------|-----|----|----|-----|----|----|----|----|----|-----|-----|------|----|-----|----|------|----|-----|
| 2012 | .348 | 55 | 50 | 207 | 44 | 72 | 13 | 7 | 5 | 59 | 114 | .551 | 19 | 0 | 36 | .401 | 7 | 7 |

# 7

# Kansas City Royals

Throughout my time at Omaha I was numerously contacted by the same Kansas City Royals scout who had been contacting me on and off for the past couple years. He explained to me that they were interested in signing me once Omaha was over and that there is a job waiting for me in Burlington North Carolina for their Rookie affiliate short season team. They were the only team to have contacted me, which I thought was odd based on the success of the season that I had. Once we returned to Tucson from Omaha, I made my decision to sign with the Royals. On June 27th I drove to Surprise, Phoenix to the Royals spring training facility. There I took a physical and signed my professional contract. My signing bonus, a mere $1,000. Despite the money, I had an opportunity, an opportunity that most people never have. The next day I drove home to San Diego to drop my car off and spend some quality time with my family for a day before I was to fly to North Carolina. Till then I hadn't been home since early January. The next day I was on a five-and-a-half-hour plane ride to Burlington North Carolina.

Nervous and excited I did not know what to expect when I got there. However, I quickly settled into a daily routine. We would practice for a few hours before getting ready for our 7:00 p.m. night games. I immediately noticed how laid back everything was and how it almost seemed like everyone would go through the motions of the practice. Some of the players were high draft picks and were given a significant amount of money. The caliber of players was talented and I knew right away that I would be able to compete with them. With the amount of knowledge I had already obtained at Arizona and coming off fresh from winning the College World Series I felt confident. The problem was that the roster was full. I was the 6th outfielder and the 3rd first baseman there. The odds were not in my favor being that I came in late because I was in Omaha. Most of these guys have had a lot of playing time already. After four days and three games I hadn't even had an at bat or played an inning on defense. The batting practice before the games were my chance to show my ability to the coaches. Despite how well I did in the practices, my manager told me I am being sent to the AZL (Arizona) League to get playing time.

As shocked as I was, I understood that this is a business and the players they have invested money in need to be played. I learned here I can be sent off anywhere at any time. So off I went on another long plane trip across the country after just being in Arizona not that long ago when I signed my contract. I flew into San Diego so that I could have my car, and then drove five hours to Phoenix. I reported to my new team and again quickly got into a routine.

I immediately noticed that the caliber of players in this league were less talented than what I saw in Burlington North Carolina. This league is mostly made up of players who signed out of high school, some junior college kids, and very young Latino players. Most of these guys had no idea what college was like and most probably will never know. I tried to not let this faze me for I saw playing in this league has an opportunity to get playing time. In my first two games I got a pinch hit at bat. The first game I grounded out but in the second game I got my first professional hit, a line drive between short stop and third base. Growing up I had always been a San Diego Padres fan and I found it fun that my first hit was against the AZL Padres. In my first career start I played first base but went 0-4 in the game. While my defense was solid, I know that my bat is what will make me move up the Minor League ladder, and going 0-4 hurts. In my second career start against the AZL Rangers I went 2-5 with a 2 RBIs. However, I did strike out my last two at bats and fouled a ball off my ankle to end my day on a poor note. Days after the game my ankle has swelled up quite significantly but I didn't dare show my trainers since it would prolong my playing time. After being there for two weeks I sensed a pattern that I will play every fourth to fifth game. Essentially my role was to give the other first baseman a rest day.

It was extremely difficult knowing I was one of the most talented players on the team but was unable to show it with my bat, sounds familiar? Some of my teammates show some promise for the future but they have a long road to becoming a polished and knowledgeable player. This is understandable considering some are seventeen and eighteen years of age. While sitting in the dugout watching the games being played, I would scratch my head multiple times asking myself, "How can this be professional baseball?" It astounded me how so many balls hit in the outfield would easily drop for a hit where in college it would be easily caught.

I even witnessed an outfielder overrun a ball that resulted in an inside the park home run. Down the right field line, the ball landed 5 feet from the foul line but the outfielder proceeded to run and hurdle the 4-foot fence into our bullpen, which was about 10 feet past the foul line. Meanwhile, the ball rolled to the wall and by the time the outfielder hurdled back over the fence the guy who hit the ball was rounding third base. The poor defense in the infield and outfield in this league shocked me because this is supposed to be professional baseball and most of these kids got drafted. I even saw a pitcher pitch a fastball and the catcher completely missed it, resulting in the ball hitting the umpire in the shoulder and shooting clear over the backstop. Some pitchers who received a significant signing bonus were wild and had a difficult time throwing strikes.

We once lost a game in the oddest way. It was the bottom of the 9th inning against the AZL Mariners. We were winning 4-2 but after a few walks and a bunt that resulted in a throwing error, the other team managed to make the score 4-3. After this, we got two outs but quickly walked a few more batters and the bases were loaded. The next batter got a base hit to left field resulting in the runner on third base easily scoring. The runner who was on second base hand no chance to score so he stopped on third base. However, the throw from the left fielder was off line to our third baseman, and he had to dive for the ball. The ball bounced out of his glove rolling to the mound. Seeing this, the runner decided to run home. Our third baseman ran to the ball and rushed his throw to the catcher. The catcher had no chance since the throw was thrown so fast and so wide. They won 5-4.

Some games were difficult to watch and play in. My first game here we gave up 16 runs in the first inning, yes 16. When I started it was usually at first base. At the University of Arizona you were expected to be vocal when you played the infield. It shocked me that when I played infield for the Royals that no one talked, it was so quiet that you could hear a pin drop. I know that being vocal on defense means that you are engaged in the game and gives the pitcher confidence so I made sure that I was vocal because that was what I was taught. I quickly learned this league is more individualized rather than team-oriented, meaning you only worry about how you do, not the team. After being on the best team in the nation, it was weird for me to experience this individualism. After a loss in college, it was expected of you to shut your mouth and not be happy but in this league, kids got away with laughing and playing around after a loss. I just wish these kids could go to college and experience how much it hurts to lose.

I am in this league because I was a free agent sign. Those who were drafted past and present had filled up the roster spots of the other teams in the Royals organization while I was at Omaha. While I truly believed my skill set and knowledge of the game far exceeded the team I was on, what matters the most is how much money is invested in you. Professional organizations like to have young players so they can develop them themselves; therefore, they are willing to fork out a lot of cash. They received the majority of the playing time and that was something I had to accept. This is similar to college baseball in that if you have scholarship money, you will play.

I had overcome the bench in college with no scholarship money so why can't I do the same in professional baseball? From experience I knew all I could do was try to stand out by hitting the ball hard all over the field, plus show that I am a hard worker when I was not starting. While my batting practices were stellar, I made sure I spent extra time in the batting cages and weight room. I know little things like that can prove to the coaches that you are a hard worker and should result in playing time. I know all too well that being in the Arizona heat can zap the enthusiasm out of a player to practice. Being used to it by now it did not faze me. I recall seeing on a regular basis our pitchers who were supposed to be shagging during batting practice find the only shade in the outfield and not move.

Every day was over 100 degrees, and it even got up to 116 degrees at times. Mental toughness is key to performing in this kind of heat. I know that if I have any hope to move up the ladder, production in the games is what truly matter. At my age of twenty-two and after all that I went through in college I knew I belonged at a higher level of play. Rookie league is for those who just got out of high school and junior college kids, not someone who was a 5th year senior out of college.

After all my hard work I failed to display my potential during the games I played in. I got myself out rather than the pitcher getting me out. The reason for this was I was trying to do too much because I expected to dominate this league. I swung at bad pitches and my timing was off. I can blame my poor performance on numerous reasons such as lack of consistent playing time, transitioning to a wood bat, but like Coach Lopez taught me, "Don't point your finger at something because three more are pointing back at you." My strikeout total almost doubled my hit total. I felt like a different person at the plate than who I was at college.

Toward the end of season, I was able to capitalize on the playing time that I had received and finished strong. The amount of extra work I put in allowed me to be more comfortable at the plate. I ended up getting 72 at bats and collected 18 hits for a batting average of .250.

Definitely not up to my standards but after a long and successful year I was ready to train and prepare myself for spring training 2013.

## Spring Training 2013

Before the beginning of spring training, which was to begin in March, I spent my off-season training and earning extra money working at an indoor hitting facility called Frozen Ropes in San Diego. I felt like I had a successful off season and was training myself mentally and physically to be ready for this journey. Partaking in Spring Training is an opportunity that not many baseball players get, and what you do in the off season will dictate how prepared you are going into Spring Training. What you are training yourself for was a month straight of baseball, no days off. You have four weeks if not sooner to prove to the organization that you belong.

Every morning the routine went as follows:

Minor League group meeting, go to your team field to stretch, practice, after practice take a lunch break, after lunch play a game, and a few times a week you were expected to complete a light strength workout. Essentially every day you would workout with the same team and play in a game with them.

The team I was on consisted of many of the same players I was with last year in the AZL. Every day it felt like there was already a plan in place as far as what team they will be sending you to after Spring Training. While you cannot control this; the only thing you can control is your performance. Teams were separated into Rookie, A, AA, AAA. While the minor leaguers were separated from the big leaguers, we did see them on a regular basis working out on fields next to us. Every day we would walk past those fields watching what we hoped to be our future. I was fortunate enough to one day do base running for the Major League team and I even met George Brett. I just remember him jokingly asking me why my last name was so long on my jersey, Fisher-Brown. Fisher-Brown was my legal last name, but I went by

Brown. I did this base running not because I had been doing so well but because it was something they had rookie ball players do on an occasional basis. While being on the same field with these MLB guys I realized some of them were my age. After doing this, I realized that I had a long way to go.

From the start of Spring Training I had been dealing with a cold that resulted in non-stop coughing for the whole month of March. The coughing was so bad at times that it affected the way I played. At the end of Spring Training I felt a small bump by my lower stomach, which I discovered later was a hernia. I had always been a healthy player, and it was generally small minor injuries that would happen to me. I thought this wasn't any different and would potentially even heal itself. Despite this, my performance during spring training was good, not excellent, but good enough in my opinion to get me out of Rookie ball. I recorded myself hitting a .300 average. However, as I stated before, there appears to be a plan already in place. Towards the last week of spring training it was not uncommon to see some players get released. I never felt worried I was going to get released, and I am sure other players felt the same, but it does happen to players you wouldn't expect. I recall all the minor leaguers anxiously waiting for the rosters to be posted on the bulletin board a few days before spring training ended. However, when that day finally came, I was not on any roster. Thankfully this did not mean I was being released, it meant I was going to be staying in Arizona for extended Spring Training, and be sent to a short season affiliate, meaning my season won't begin for another two and a half months until June.

## Extended Spring Training

The number of players involved in extended spring training was big enough to make two full teams. The routine generally stayed the same. Practice in the early morning, and play a game against another organizations extended team in the late morning. At that time, I worked a lot with the outfield group. I felt like I would get more opportunity playing outfield because there were always three spots to fill and I could show off my speed. The summer before I only played first base, a position I always felt the most natural at. Picking balls in the dirt and moving around the bag was generally easy for me. It was this position that I once felt like was going to be the place for me to excel when I was at the University of Arizona but it never came about. It wasn't until the coaches at Arizona gave other players more opportunity at first base that I felt obligated to move myself to the outfield. While being in the outfield during extended spring training I will admit I wasn't the best. Others took better routes and had a stronger arm than me. Our outfield coach even one day told us straight up who the top 4 outfielders were out of the 8 of us, I wasn't one of them. It is hard to admit but he was right. It wasn't until after this moment that I started asking the coaches to give me some work at first base. I knew I was better and way more experienced than the ones who had been working out there.

All us players in extended Spring Training were warned that any of us can move up to one of the long season teams at any moment. It is a long season and players get hurt. While this is also based off luck that a player who plays the same position as you at the A, AA, or AAA level got hurt, the players that performed the best were the ones chosen to move up. It did happen sometimes that players got moved up in the middle of the extended Spring Training, but it wasn't occurring on a regular basis. My performance was again good, but not standout great. I would at least get one hit every game that I played in but what I was not showing was my power. What these coaches liked seeing was the ball being driven deep in the outfield. While I look back on this now, I wonder if I should have changed my hitting approach. My approach was always to hit the ball gap to gap, and/or hit a low line drive. At the University of Arizona, we were not taught to try to hit the ball out of the park because we played on such a big field. I had always had easy power to drive the ball over the fence but I never tried to because physically trying to do this causes inconsistent swings, which result in a lower average.

A moment that stood out among the rest over the two and a half months was when one morning every player involved in extended spring training was forced to do punishment running because of something that had happened at the team hotel. We got word that some of the Latin players were acting up at the hotel, and because not one of the Latin players admitted to what he had done we were all forced to run. All of about 50 of us lined up on the line and ran ten yards up, then back, then back again. This doesn't sound that bad until you have done it about 40 times straight. While this is something I can expect in college, I never would have expected this in professional baseball. I strongly feel the coaches that authorized this abused their power, and went about this completely wrong. A few players even hurt their hamstrings after doing this. I had already felt the start of a hernia in my lower stomach before this was happening, and this certainly made it worse. I was naive to think that the hernia would go away, but at that time I felt I needed to tough it out.

Early June was the Major League Draft. From a minor leaguer's perspective this is the time of the year when you feel uncomfortable because you know you are going to soon encounter some new competition and possibly soon be released. This was the reality that we lived in and players did get released to make room for the new players. For my competition, the Royals drafted a hand full of first basemen and outfielders who would soon be making their way to the Surprise, Arizona where we had all been for the last three and a half months from the start of Spring Training. Yes, I was uneasy about the new crop of players coming in whilst being anxious at this point to just start my season. The newly drafted players who signed found themselves at the tail end of our extended spring training, about a week before we were to be sent to our Short Season Affiliate team. During this time, I remember the rosters for the teams being posted on the same board where we did not see our names back in March. There were three teams now, the AZL Royals that I played on last summer, the Burlington Royals, and Idaho Falls Chuckers. My team was the Burlington Royals, the same place where I spent 4 days and didn't play last year.

## Burlington Royals

From all my time playing for the Royals, I would say that I enjoyed my time the most playing in Burlington, North Carolina. This was where I received the most playing time, and often found myself hitting 3rd or 4th in the lineup. We were in the Appalachian League, playing against teams in nearby towns and states. Our field in Burlington was by far the best maintained field in the league. There were some fields that were downright dangerous to play on, and we were at least fortunate to play on a flat field for our home games. There was one time while fielding ground balls before a game at an opposing teams' field where a ball took a bad hop bouncing straight up into my sunglasses cracking them. These towns that we traveled to were small, in the middle of nowhere, but they still yielded a big turnout of fans. The fans in this league were passionate about their home town team, and it reminded me of college.

Bobby Brown, left, of the Burlington Royals reaches home plate after a solo home run — his first homer since the 2012 College World Series — and is greeted by teammate Alfredo Escalera on Saturday night at Burlington Athletic Stadium.

First he's watching from the dugout, by the end of the night he becomes ... **Downtown Brown**

**Royals produce first 3-0 start to season**

While there was another first baseman named Sam Bates competing for playing time with me, we both found a decent amount of playing time in the form of one would play first base, while the other would DH. For a short time, the both of us were being nicknamed the 'Bash Bros.' I was even called 'Downtown Brown.' Sam and I became good friends during our time in Burlington, he would even be a groomsman at my wedding years later in 2015. We were both hosted by the Strigo family who treated us very well, and made us some amazing meals that summer. While Sam showcased more of his power throughout the season, I did find ourselves as being pretty similar players. I prided myself on playing great defense. I only committed 3 errors on the season in 246 innings played. However, as I stated before, it comes down to how you swing the bat. I certainly had some great moments. I hit my first professional home run off a pinch hit at bat, and even in the same game in the next at bat got a walk off hit. In practice, I showcased my power and ability to drive the ball to all parts of the field. Many times, I was complimented from my teammates on how well I swung. As I know, being a good batting practice hitter doesn't mean you will showcase the same in the game, it only shows what you are capable of.

I finished the season with 27 hits in 149 at bats, batting the lowest I have ever in my life, .181, with 4 home runs, and 18 RBIs. I simply could not get it going on a consistent basis. I remember one three game series where I went 0-12 and lined out to the center fielder 10 times, it was that kind of season. Bad luck, bad timing, excuses don't matter. The stats are what they are. While it was very difficult for me to be accept my failure, it took a long time for me to realize the cause. It was not too long after the season was over that I ended up getting released, and thus ending my baseball career. It was a tough call to take, certainly scripted, and to the point. Though you might think that I would have been emotional, I was not. I was almost relieved and the next chapter will explain why. I hope that my failure can turn into your success for those of you that are looking to play professionally one day.

# 8

# What I Learned

My relief stems from the fact that I had accomplished what most have not. I was at the point in my life that I felt ready to move on. Perhaps this is the same mentality I had always had as a player – The ability to move on to what I need to do next. I felt the need to write this book so that I can tell aspiring baseball players, parents, and coaches that it is worth it. It is worth putting the time and money into a player's baseball development because they will get so much more out of it than just the fundamentals. Baseball really does teach you about life. Do I feel that I had the ability to play in the Major Leagues? Yes, I do. It did not happen, so I must do what baseball has taught me – Learn from the failure and move on. Maybe I am like the typical jock having a high view point of my ability, but I do believe everything happens for a reason.

There are many things that I learned while playing baseball that can aid any player looking to make a career in baseball. First off, I am glad that my parents pushed me to play professionally. I can forever have on my resume that I had the opportunity to be in the Major Leagues. It is a difficult feat to get to where I got, and one that stems from hard work at an early age. Here I have put together valuable tips that I hope will help you from my playing career, and time as a coach. The best way to explain everything to you players, dads, and coaches, is bullet pointed below:

At any point do not take this game too seriously. Remember that baseball is supposed to make you fail. Take everything step by step.

When a kid shows some promise seek out professional training from qualified coaches. Don't be afraid to try to push your child to get better.

At a young age a player needs to learn the basic fundamentals of hitting, throwing, fielding, and catching. I often see players know how to hit a ball before they can throw it properly.

At any level a player must be mentally tough. It is hard to accept failure, but learning from your failure will only make you a better baseball player.

If you plan on seeking out a travel ball team, do not feel obligated to be on the best team in the region. Yes, players should be challenged but what is more important is for that player to get playing time and have a positive experience. Negative experience results in players not bringing out their true potential.

Realize that at a young age you are preparing your player/child to make their high school freshman team. If they go beyond their freshman team, it is an added bonus.

If your child/player shows promise in high school then this is the time they need to be working harder than ever to get a collegiate scholarship. Anything better than this, aka getting drafted, is an added bonus.

It is often in high school where it is easy for a player to get distracted by other things, taking away from their potential, for example: Girls and Social Media. Parents and coaches need to help guide these players on a path to success.

Do not think that because your child did not get that Division 1 Scholarship that they won't play professionally one day. A very small percentage of baseball collegiate athletes get even a partial scholarship. Many players get drafted out of Division 2, or Junior Colleges.

There are many collegiate options, and I think it is important you do your research before accepting to play for a certain college. The research entails seeing who has received a scholarship to play there, who has a scholarship that is currently there, and what were their recent stats.

When a player is in college it is important that they stay focused on what matters. Being away from home for the first time is an important experience, and yes you should have fun, but know that I have seen many talented players ruin their potential to getting drafted because they had too much fun.

When you are in college, and truly desire to be drafted you must out work, out hustle, outperform the competition. Realize that in college most of the players are of equal, if not better in terms of the talent they possess.

Like in high school, in college take advantage of your playing time. Do not be afraid to communicate to your coaches what you need to work on, and how you can get more playing time.

There is certainly a social game that is played in baseball between coaches and players, and the earlier you realize this the better. Coaches will have their favorites, but even if you are not the most vocal, you can be very loud in your playing performance.

Practice with a wood bat at a young age. Good hitters can feel the difference, and will only better prepare you for the next level.

Be realistic and make sure you have a plan B in college. You might not get drafted, so having a degree is something you may need to fall back on.

Know that if you have the opportunity to play professional baseball, you should take it. The opportunity will only come around once in a lifetime.

Once in professional baseball the only thing you can control is your performance. A lot of the players that are in the big leagues are there because of luck, and timing. But of course, they are all gifted.

Playing in the Minor Leagues is a grind, and I only got a small taste of it. You must truly love the game to get through the grind. It is an opportunity of a lifetime, so take advantage of it.

Remember that this is just a game, play it like you would do it for free, like the time you did as a kid.

Lastly, there is life after baseball. Do not be afraid to seek out another passion, if your career did not end up the way you wanted.

# 9

# Overcoming the Bench

Most of my college career was spent on the bench. During my 5 years at Arizona I experienced many highs and many lows from the bench. I would sit there in the dugout game after game and know that I would not be even considered for a pinch hit at bat. All I could do while sitting there was hope that my chance would come and that if it did, then I'd take full advantage of it. There were times that I did get my opportunity and I was successful, and there were times that I was unsuccessful. "How I overcame all this?" This is a hard question to answer. In my head I always knew that I was a good player because I have constantly been successful my whole life. Somehow, I always felt like my chance would eventually come and I would turn out to be an everyday starter. If someone was to tell me I was going to be in college for 5 years and spend most of it on the bench, I would have said, "You are crazy."

What I have learned from sitting on the bench I would say had helped me finish my college career positively. During my 5 years, game after game I would observe everything that was going on. I would watch the other team and imagine myself hitting in certain situations and coming up with a big hit to help the team win. Even in batting practice I would see myself coming up to the plate and driving some runs in. I believe this is why most of my career pinch hit at bats have been successful for me. Baseball is mostly mental as most people know. As long as your state of mind is positive on the bench then you are setting yourself up for success. Now I'll admit my state of mind was not always positive when I sat all those games. After some games, I would ask myself, "What am I doing here? I never play." As difficult as it was, I knew that being mentally tough would get me through it.

There were times that I got a pinch hit at bat and I got a big hit but I wouldn't get another opportunity for a few weeks. I was confused and upset, and I tried to hide it as much as I could. By hiding my emotions, I thought the coaches would notice I wasn't upset, and it would lead to playing time. However, by hiding my emotions it made me extremely quiet. I did not realize this early in my career but I learned that it is important to always be vocal on the bench and make sure your coaches notice you because it will increase your odds of coming into the game. My quiet nature certainly hurt my odds of playing, but then again, I always thought I could let my bat do the talking.

My advice to any aspiring college baseball player would be to always support your teammates whether you are playing or not. Once you get an opportunity to play make sure you are prepared for it, which will allow you to take advantage of it. Visualizing being successful while not playing can only make you feel more confident for when that opportunity arises. It is important to prove to your teammates and coaches that you are 100 percent devoted to the team and earn their respect. If you show them you work your butt off, and are a good teammate on and off the field, there is no doubt your opportunity will come. Being on the bench is not easy but you can't use that as an excuse to pout and whine because you don't want to miss that opportunity.

# 10

# Being A Student Athlete

Playing a sport for a Division 1 school is by no means easy. If it was easy, everyone would do it. No one really knows how to handle the stress of being a student athlete unless you have done it yourself. This makes the small percentage of student athletes in the United States so unique. You have to learn how to manage your time and keep your priorities straight, because if you cannot, then being a student athlete is not right for you. Most people do not understand the amount of time and commitment it takes. Like most student athletes, I had to adjust to waking up sometimes at 5:00 a.m. or 6:00 a.m. to go weight lift and/or for conditioning. Some days I felt like I was going to pass out but what drove me to complete it was being in top physical shape. You have to learn to love weight lifting on a regular basis because those who couldn't handle it wouldn't make the team.

After this, I had to find a quick breakfast and go to class. Usually the classes I took either lasted from 9:00 a.m. to 1:00 p.m. or 9:30 a.m. to 1:45 p.m. depending on the day. In between the classes I found time for lunch. Next was practice that always started at 2:30 p.m. but sometimes I'd get there early to get extra hitting practice. Practice usually lasted three hours. After practice, I found dinner and had to find the motivation to do homework after a long day of work. With many days like this you can imagine how this is not for everyone and how many athletes can't handle it. Doing this forces many student athletes to grow up quickly, but as I have seen from experience many don't want to. Some embrace the lifestyle change and some don't, but those that do are bound for more success.

I have witnessed firsthand many baseball players who have a tremendous amount of talent but lack the desire to do well in the classroom, and don't work hard in practice and the weight room. All athletes come into college with a high expectation of being the best and they think college will be a walk in the park. Quickly for some, they are overwhelmed and homesick. As for others, they embrace the student athlete lifestyle and feel the need to succeed. All that hard work will pay off one day, I guarantee it. After working my butt off for years in college and not playing, all that hard work paid off when I became an everyday starter in my senior year. All those long hours of writing papers and going to class paid off when I finally received my degree. Going through all those tough times and long days that sometimes seemed like they would never end was well worth it and has made me a better person. All my blood, sweat, and tears from 5 years of college led me to a National Championship. I am one of the few who can say I have a College World Series ring and I will always wear it with pride. Every time I look at it, it reminds me of all the tough times and how I overcame it. Go to college and enjoy every minute of it.

While some choose the college path, others get drafted out of high school and sign professionally. Some Latin American players even sign professionally when they are sixteen years old. From all that I have seen and experienced I would recommend going to college over signing out of high school. Sure, every kid has a different situation, and sometimes there is money offered to you that you just can't refuse. However, signing out of high school takes the college experience away. College is a chance to be away from home for the first time and be independent. College is an opportunity to earn a degree, and meet lifelong friends. Many can't handle being away from home and find the experience too overwhelming. Like most kids, I would not have been prepared to play professionally right out of high school. Going to college allowed me to grow up and enhance my skills and knowledge of the game. I don't believe the majority of high school players who got drafted have a strong knowledge of how to play the game the right way. With that being said, it is rare for professional baseball players to have a long career in the Minors, especially in the Major Leagues. Every year players get cut and/or retire from the game. These young men must now accept a life without baseball and start a new chapter in their lives. Most do not have a college degree forcing them to either go back to school or get a job that doesn't require a degree. I'm saddened by those who signed out of high school and find themselves out of the game later in their mid-twenties. If they had just gone to college and completed at least 3 years of school, they could have easily gone back and finished. The reality is that few will make it to the big leagues and at some point, they will have to do something else.

Major League Baseball should follow the footsteps of basketball and football and require kids to go to college before getting drafted. This could only be positive for professional baseball, if you break it down. Playing college baseball will allow players to mature and learn how to actually compete for a starting position. Collegiate baseball is not easy at any level; some conferences such as the PAC 12 and SEC are even considered to be just as good or even better than AA professional baseball. Many young players out of high school believe they are "the guy" and haven't ever competed against someone for a job in the starting line-up or starting rotation. Once they become a student-athlete, competition will surely prove if they can handle that pressure. This is because if they get to the Major Leagues, of course, someone is always competing for your job. If professional baseball organizations want to build a strong farm system with better caliber of players, as in players who are more mature and understand how to play the game, then they need to draft college players. It blows my mind to see so many talented college players get passed on the draft for some young high school player. These high school players deserve a chance to be a student-athlete, and better yet, get an education and have the opportunity to compete for a National Championship like I did.

# 11

# Dealing With Failure

I have learned over the course of my baseball life that if you really want to make this your career, you have to love the game. Many of us men have grown up playing and watching the game, perhaps even dreaming of making it to the big time. We grow up playing catch with dad, going to the batting cages, and learning how to field a ground ball. Those are the golden days in my opinion since baseball is fun. Ask any young little leaguer between the ages of five and eight, what they think about the game and I would bet you they would say, "It's fun," or "I love it." There is a point in every boy's life where baseball is not fun anymore. The reality is that 99 percent of us will not even come close to making the Major Leagues.

One issue with baseball especially as a kid is the tremendous amount of failure we all experience. Some of us grow up with raw talent that helps give us an edge but nevertheless we all encounter failure. If you have played this game and do not love it, it's perhaps because you did not enjoy the failure. Failure is just part of the game, plain and simple. Getting over that failure and using it to your advantage is another story. The more you fail, the harder you have to work in the game of baseball. This goes for life as well, not just baseball. The beauty about the game is that it can teach you about life, if you are paying attention.

I hear this way too often, "Kids are getting softer and softer." You cannot have success in baseball unless you overcome the failure. When something gets hard you fight even harder to overcome it. Don't be soft and let the failure consume you. So many kids give up this love for the game because of the failure. Giving up on the game as a kid because you make a lot of errors or strike out a lot is soft. Baseball cannot ever be perfected; it takes years and years of hard work to improve skills necessary to be good at the game. No one, not even professionals have perfected the game. The few boys that truly love this game will beg their dad to throw batting practice, want the best instruction they can find, and work on a skill when they have down time. It is so difficult to do this as a child because society is shouting at them to play video games, and sit on the couch and watch television. There is nothing wrong if a kid wants to explore other sports. Of course, baseball is not for everyone.

If baseball was easy, everyone would be doing it. You have to remember, getting 3 hits out of 10 at bats means you are a great hitter. In order to deal with this failure, it is important to focus on the successes you have had. Instead of thinking about your recent strike out or error, think back to a recent good at bat or great defensive play you made. So much of our mind is littered with negative thoughts. We must clear our minds and focus on something positive. For example: If you are a hitter, instead of thinking, "I can't get a hit. All I do is hit it right at someone," think, "I am going to hit this ball in the gap." If you are pitcher, instead of thinking, "I don't want to walk this person," think, "I will locate this ball on the corner." Failures cause troubling thoughts to engulf our brains, but shifting your own negative thoughts while performing to positive thoughts can only help you succeed.

During my National Championship season in 2012 me and my teammates met with a Sports Psychologist named Greg Warburton. At first it seemed like our meeting with him was odd but after we won the National Championship, I remember thinking, "Did that meeting with Greg help us win the National Championship." Strangely, I think, "Yes." I believe that everything happens for a reason, and this meeting was supposed to happen.

Greg met with us during the weekend of March 23rd–25th while we were playing at Oregon State. Greg discussed various aspects of the mental part of the game from his e-book *Peak Performance Mental Game: Stay in The Zone Using EFT*. Greg believes that by tapping the EFT points on the body, it boosts energy, enhances focus, and address's mental blocks to peak performance. EFT stands for 'Emotional Freedom Technique.' The points to tap on the body include the sternum, underarm, and parts of the face and hand. What I believe the tapping does is relaxes the mind, essentially making you forget the negatives of the game. From his handout, Peak Performance Mental Game Fast-Start Guide, Greg explains, "In a nutshell, all you really have to do is to put your total attention on your mind and body. All you are looking to become aware of is whether or not you feel stressed and hesitant or relaxed and ready. If you notice stress, then you tap for whatever is on your mind and in your body." While at the time he was telling us this and showing how to do this I remember seeing the strange look in my teammate's faces. I myself questioned why we were doing this, but I have always been to open to new things.

I am not 100 percent certain how many of my teammates continued using this tapping technique for the remainder of the season. I did it occasionally, perhaps stemming from being a superstitious baseball player. However, what I do believe is he did help us. He talked about shifting your mental thought process to focus on how you do want to perform. For example, tell yourself, "I will hit the ball hard up the middle," instead of, "I will strike out." In order to do this, you have to be honest with yourself on what your thoughts are during the game. After hearing this, I understood that my thoughts were not always positive.

Before this weekend series I had been struggling a bit to start the season, and even sat for a few games. What came with this failure to start the season were negative thoughts. After this series, I didn't sit for the rest of the year and I cannot recall sensing too much negativity. I even ended up hitting my first career college home run that weekend against Oregon State.

Unfortunately, my grandfather had passed away that same weekend. I wasn't told this until after the series since my family didn't want it to be a distraction. When I hit that ball, I felt for sure it would just go into the right center gap and it would most likely be a double. However, it managed to carry over the fence as if I got a little extra help. Whether it was a coincidence or not, nevertheless it was a confidence booster.

You can often tell when a player has failed by their body language. Shoulders are hunched, head and chest are down. While we all know that this is a game of failure, we have to understand how to deal with it. I understand as a former player that when you are not performing well it's hard not to wear those emotions on your sleeve. When I was playing well, I felt a sense of control and trust. The book *Heads-Up Baseball: Playing The Game One Pitch At A Time* by Ken Ravizza and Tom Hanson goes into details on the subject of how to deal with failure. Along the same lines from what Greg Warburton was trying to get across, the book explains, "A simple and effective way to regain control is to carry yourself as if you were extremely confident and in control. Thinking confident thoughts makes you feel confident; carrying yourself in a confident way does the same thing." When you play well it increases your focus. When your focus has increased you are in control of the game one pitch at a time.

Sometimes all it takes is for a good at bat or a good weekend series to get you going offensively. When you're not going well you must not forget to focus on, "playing one pitch at a time," as the book explains. The process of playing one pitch at a time is self-control, plan your performance, and trust. "Only when under control can you think clearly about what to do next, and only when under control can you give up control and get to trust." I interpret this process of playing one pitch at a time as being "in the zone." Being in the zone is something that athletes experience as a temporary mastery of a skill. When you are in the zone you feel mentally calm, self-confident, and in control. Regardless, if you are in the zone or not, simply carry yourself confidently as if you are. Your chances of accomplishing your task increases when you do so.

# 12

# "The Game"

Imagine the game of baseball as an invisible person. This person who we shall properly call "the game" feeds off of your negative energy. "The game" enjoys putting pressure on you when times are tough, and rewards those with poise and confidence. Those who work hard to improve their ability are more likely to not encounter this mysterious person we call "the game." Those who panic and have the inability to slow the game down in a pressure situation are prone to becoming best friends with "the game." "The game," will psychologically try to intimidate and distract you from being in that focused state of mind.

Where "the game" can get controlled is at practice. It is so easy to go through the motions of practice especially when you do the same thing every day. Drills become repetitive and boring, making it easy to lose focus. This is where "the game" likes to jump in and attack, or in other words expose you. I have been a victim to this attack more than once in my life. First you lose focus, then you get exposed, and then you are just embarrassed. Having the ability to block out "the game" is no easy task, but those who can do this, being mentally tough in games and in practice, will come to find that baseball gets a lot easier and less stressful. "The game" is of course your own mind.

"The game" is a phrase I have borrowed from Coach Lopez, my head coach at the University of Arizona, and it was engrained in my head for 5 years. The game of baseball is much more mental than physical. Yogi Berra once said humorously, "Eighty percent of the game is half mental." Well Yogi is right in an odd way. This game is much more mental than physical. So much of the game is spent standing around, especially when the ball never comes toward you. No position is least likely to have a ball hit your way than outfield at a young age. You are surrounded by a sea of grass, far away from the home plate. The outfield is almost like a strange world where you can get lost in your own mind. It is so easy to get distracted and lose focus. Why do you think you see little leaguers with their short attention spans bending down picking the grass during a game? And just when they lose that focus, guess who the ball gets hit to? Baseball is unique in that way and no other sport is like it. The mental part of the game is what makes baseball the hardest game to play, hands down.

While you have many goals as a coach one should be making sure that your team can stay focused for the entire game. Whether the game is only an hour and a half or three hours, you can't let your team lose that focus for even an inning. Remember "the game" is always around and while all players are susceptible to encountering it, little leaguers are especially vulnerable.

Now how do you as a coach eliminate "the big inning" or multiple errors? My answer to that is the well-known phrase, "Practice makes perfect." While you make your practice plans, keep in mind that you want your players to know what to do with the ball before it is hit to them. Practice game situations repeatedly and make sure you run your practices at the same tempo as a game. If your players are used to a slow practice tempo, then when it comes game time everything is too fast. When the game is too fast their mental confidence lowers, hence "the game" is there.

Why is it that after many games as a coach you scratch your head and wonder: "If only we didn't have that one bad inning?" While you are frustrated that certain kids made errors or the pitcher walked a bunch of hitters, don't forget you are partially at fault as well. Yes, errors will happen and there is nothing you can do about it. You can only control what you can control. What you control is raising each individual player's confidence and skill level. This all starts in practice. Putting more emphasis on mechanics and technique while being energetic and a good communicator is part of your job. It brings a positive mentality for when the games start. So, before you put the blame on individual kids think about whether you spent enough time on the parts of the game that caused your team to lose. If you have spent a considerable amount of time on a particular skill and the individual player is still not getting it, understand patience and more repetition is needed.

# 13

# Coaching

## Philosophy

Looking back on all the great coaches I have had in my life they all had common traits. Confident, well spoken, and organized. A line I will borrow from Coach Andy Lopez is, "Have a plan, get them ready, and play the right guys." This philosophy is something I have adopted. From the time that I was in high school playing for Coach Sam Blalock to the time going into college at Arizona with Coach Andy Lopez I always noticed an organized practice itinerary was there. These coaches had a plan.

Practices were always upbeat and they had a good way of expressing how they wanted something to be done so that it was natural when we played in a game. These coaches got us ready. The toughest task I found in this philosophy is playing the right guys. Putting the right 9 guys in defensive positions or places in the line-up is not the simplest of tasks. It's all about putting kids in the spots you think will set the team up for success.

All teams have A, B, and C level players. 'A' players are the most talented and usually consist of 2 or 3 kids on the roster. 'B' players are the majority of the team, and are the average players. 'C' players are the least talented kids, and usually consist of 2 or 3 players like the 'A' players. Everyone has heard of the phrase, "You are only as good as your weakest link." What I am getting at here is that as coaches we need to spend more time getting the 'C' players up to 'B' level, and make one or two of the 'B' players into 'A' players. With the proper amount of time and attention to detail, this can be accomplished, and you will watch the team succeed.

## Travel Ball

If you believe your child needs more of a challenge, then get him or her involved in travel ball. Travel teams are generally comprised of all-star caliber players who play similar teams in the same city or town you live. The benefits of travel ball are the better coaching and higher competition level. But be warned, the politics you see in little league are still there in travel ball.

The problem with little league is you generally get inexperienced dads coaching. Often, you will see "daddy ball" where their son gets most of the playing time and makes the

all-star team even though he wasn't the best player on the team. Practices are not fast paced, energetic, instructional, and fun. While this is not necessarily the fault of the dad who was nice enough to volunteer his services, the fault can be blamed on the Little League board members for not following through on their head coaches being taught the right coaching techniques and fundamentals of the game. Unfortunately, little leagues seem to neglect this which causes kids to fade away from the game at an early age. The percentage of kids that drop out of youth sports by the age of thirteen are staggering. The National Alliance for Sports report that, "70% of these kids quit playing these league sports by age 13." The reason for this is that it stopped being fun. What this tells us? This is not just a Little League issue; it is a national youth sports issue across America. Unfortunately, the older the player gets, the less teams there are.

What I have seen through observing many little league practices is that there is too much standing around. Kids attention spans are short, inactivity causes them to lose interest. This inactivity leads to a lack of improvement, translating to poor play in the game. The poor play in the games causes frustration among the parents and coaches resulting in the kid putting more pressure on himself or herself to perform. Little Leagues need to do a better job of educating their coaches so that the percentage of drop outs decrease. While this may never change the best alternative is to join a travel baseball team.

I am not saying that all travel ball teams have great coaching. However, you will find more often than not, the practices are fast paced, energetic, instructional, and fun. Playing time is often not given, it is earned. You will see the improvement and enthusiasm level for the game rise. Since many of these teams stay together for longer than a year, these kids become lifelong friends. Whereas in little league you are with the same team for only 4 months. I had the time of my life playing on travel teams. Traveling to play in tournaments with my friends and competing to play in the championship game will always be a cherished memory. If your son or daughter is one of the 70 percent who dropped out of youth sports, you can still rekindle that passion. Seek out travel teams and watch as your child finds new love for the game.

## Elbow Up Epidemic

Please stop teaching "elbow up." Throughout my time coaching I started noticing a trend among many youth parent coaches, they like to use the phrase "elbow up." This inherently means "elbow above the shoulder." There are two reasons why this phrase keeps getting used. Firstly, the phrase is used because fathers were told this by their father growing up. Secondly, there is a belief that it will make it easier for the player to hold their bat up. The problem with "elbow up" is that it is taught to be too high. You will not be able to have your fingers properly lined up, if your elbow is too high. While every Major League player has their so called "style" when in their batting stance, and it might look cool when they do it, it doesn't mean it is a correct form to teach. You must remember that Major League players have incredible eye hand coordination, which is better than 99.9 percent of the population, and this talent makes up for some flaws.

There needs to be a set standard as to how high youth player's elbows should be when learning how to hit. My philosophy is to keep the elbow below the height of the shoulder but not by the ribs. My reasoning behind this is when a hitter gets to the "knob to ball" position, the elbow needs to be close to the rib cage, hence the lower the elbow the less time it takes for the elbow to be by the rib cage. The quicker a hitter can get to the ball the better, especially with how much faster pitchers are throwing nowadays. I also find with most youth hitters who have been taught "elbow up" or mimic certain pro hitters, they tend to drop their back shoulder upon trying to take the "knob to ball," causing the hitter to swing up.

## Launch Angle Epidemic

There are a lot of fun statistics being thrown around now with the advancements in technology. However, the one that needs to be stopped is "launch angle." Coaches and scouts are becoming obsessed with this. The thought is: If you have a proper launch angle, you can increase your chances of hitting home runs. While yes, this is true, it doesn't mean that players should be practicing this. I have witnessed players who have been taught this technique and I hear the same thing over and over, "My son cannot get on base anymore, he just hits pop ups." There is so much added pressure nowadays to hit the ball over the fence that other stats such as batting average and on base percentage seem less meaningful. We might not see many true great hitters anymore like Tony Gwynn, Pete Rose, and Ichiro Suzuki, players who made a living putting the ball in play rather than trying to put the ball over the fence.

Their needs to be more emphasis on hitting line drives, which is more realistic to teach players how to do. When a hitter swings level it increases their chance of hitting the ball. This will inevitably raise the confidence levels of youth hitters, which will increase the odds of them wanting to stay in the game. When a hitter swings up it decreases their chances of making contact and if they do, it will commonly be either a pop up, foul ball, or swing and miss. While hitting home runs are fun, not everyone, especially the youth, are strong enough to do it. A combination of the lack of coaching from little leagues, and the new "launch angle" craze, is leading to less kids wanting to play the game. It is Major League Baseball's responsibility to be promoting the proper fundamentals and techniques to youth players and they are failing at this by pushing "launch angle" as the right way to swing.

# 14

# Mechanics of the swing

Not everyone is blessed with a natural ability to hit a baseball. The hardest thing to do in any sport is to swing a bat at a moving ball. The mechanics of the swing are very complex, and not even the current players in the Major League have perfected it. Those that are in the Major Leagues are the ones who can consistently repeat the correct mechanics of the swing. Even for them they have to constantly practice their swing because all it takes is one minor incorrect movement to throw off the whole swing. Practicing correct habits are the key, but not everyone has that eye to see the flaw.

As a parent, when teaching your child to swing you can more than likely see that something doesn't look right, but can you see the root cause of the problem? If you see the root cause, can you explain it in a way that makes sense, and without you and your child getting frustrated? Now, if you explained it the right way, can your son or daughter now feel the bad habit and feel what the correct habit should be?

Over my time as a player and coach I have learned that there are 5 steps of the swing. These steps are by no means simple, but what I have done is provided you dad's and coaches with a complete breakdown of the swing to help you get the most out of your sons or daughters ability. Some players will have that natural ability to do these steps well. However, it is those that work tirelessly at all 5 of these steps that have the most success in this game. Every player, regardless of talent, will need to work on all 5 steps to be a consistent hitter.

# 1) Stance

As a coach I see many young kids in an un-athletic stance. I always start by looking at their hands to see, if their knuckles are lined up. To see if their knuckles are lined up have them hold their bat and point their index fingers straight out. If the fingers line up, then have them close their fingers and check their grip. Gripping the bat with medium pressure is important for the hands to have freedom of movement. A grip that is too light or too tight will throw off their setup for contact. The hands should be raised above the back shoulder. The bat should be tilted around a 45-degree angle so that the knob of the bat is facing the catcher's feet. Next have him or her spread their feet out slightly wider than their shoulders and make sure the toes are lined up. The knees should be bent so that they can feel their toes and not their heels. Both eyes need to be looking straight ahead at the pitcher. Lastly, 60 percent of their weight should be on their back leg, with 40 percent on their front.

### Check List:

✓ Knuckles lined up;

✓ Medium grip;

✓ Hands raised shoulder height;

✓ Knob tilted towards catcher;

✓ Feet spread out slightly wider than shoulder length;

✓ Knees bent;

✓ Both eyes on the pitcher;

✓ 60 percent of their weight on back leg, 40 percent on front.

## 2) Load & Stride

Loading is the most common step of the swing that I see done incorrectly. Kids tend to make this more complicated than it really is. Many kids tend to lose control of their top hand and let the barrel fall behind them. The hands should go back slightly at the same time the front foot takes a small step forward. The hands are already back, and there is no reason to make a big movement. Try to avoid having your player drop or raise their hands. To help with this tell your player to keep the knob pointed at the catcher's feet. The front foot should again land forward straight ahead. Too big of a step will cause the weight to transfer to the front leg and throw off the timing. Remember that 60 percent of the weight is still on the back leg. Lastly, the head does not raise, lower, or twist.

### Check List:

✓ Hands go back slightly;

✓ Front foot takes a small step forward;

✓ Knob is still pointed to the catcher's feet;

✓ Weight is still 60 percent on back leg, 40 percent on front leg;

✓ Head stays on the same plane.

## 3) Knob to the Ball

After loading the hands back, now it is time for the hands to make their way towards the ball. The player should now pull the knob of the bat across their chest straight out to the inner part of the ball. At the same time the back hip has started to rotate and the back foot is almost fully pivoted. Therefore, the upper body and lower body work in unison. The hands arc going to the inside of the ball so that contact will happen on the back of the ball. A common mistake is to open up the front shoulder. This is called, "pulling off the ball." The opposite of this is for the hands to travel to the outside of the ball, which is also called "casting out." Casting out will cause the top hand to roll over resulting in a ground ball and or a foul ball. You want your player to be "short and quick" to the ball as the saying goes. The longer their swing, the longer it takes to get to the ball. As the knob is pulling the barrel should be slightly above the hands. If the barrel is under the hands, the tendency is to swing up. If the barrel is too high, the tendency is to swing too steep. The reason the barrel is slightly above the hands is to generate back spin on the ball. The back hip is going to generate the torque and power. Lastly, the head will again stay still.

### Check List:

✓ Knob pulls to inside of the ball as it is close to the chest;

✓ Barrel is slightly above the hands;

✓ Back hip has started to rotate;

✓ The back foot is almost fully pivoted;

✓ Head stays still.

## 4) Contact

The hands are now prepared for contact. The top hand will now lead the "snap" to the back of the ball. Remember the knob was pulled to inside of the ball so that contact will happen on the back of the ball. Back in the first step I told you to have a medium grip on the bat. Now that your player is at the contact position the hands should squeeze as it is "snapping" to the ball. Contact should always be out front of the body no matter where the pitch is located. The inside pitch will be the pitch where contact is most out front of the body, where the outside is the least out front. Nevertheless, contact needs to be out front. I tell those that I coach to, "not let the ball beat you to the front of the plate." The hand position at contact should be, "palm up, palm down." This means the top hand faces up and the bottom hand faces down. The back foot is now fully pivoted and the hips are now facing the pitcher. The weight needs to still be back on their back leg. The front leg should be straight. Use the phrase "drive the back knee into the front knee." If you notice that their front knee is bent forward, then he or she didn't keep their weight back. Lastly, the eyes should, "watch contact." If you look at the video of almost all major leaguers, you will notice that at contact their head is down on the ball. Every step that I have discussed involves little to no head movement. This is the key for the eyes to recognize the speed of the pitch.

### Check List:

✓ Snap the top hand at the ball while squeezing both hands;

✓ Palm up, palm down;

✓ Contact out front of body;

✓ Weight back;

✓ Back foot is fully pivoted and hips face the pitcher;

✓ Eyes on contact.

## 5) Finish the Swing High

After contact, it is important that your player gets their arms extended and finishes the swing next to the front shoulder. A key phrase that I use for all players I coach is, "go through the ball." If your player finishes the swing low by their front hip, then he or she did not get good extension. This is also the point where many young players have trouble with balance. To test balance, have your player keep their head and eyes at the same point of contact and don't move for two seconds after the bat hits the shoulder.

### Check List:

✓ Extend through the ball;

✓ Keep the head and eyes at the same point of contact;

✓ The bat hits their shoulder.

Because baseball and softball is a game of failure, remember that your son or daughter can do all 5 of these steps well during an at bat and not get a hit. However, consistently performing these 5 steps well during an at bat will yield results. It is significant that you find a way to explain these mechanics in a way your son or daughter understands. Most importantly, he or she needs to *feel* the correct way to swing. Lastly, this is not the sport where you can take time off and it's like riding a bike when you start back up. Work on these mechanics with your son or daughter year-round and you will be amazed at their progression as the years go by.

# 15

# Being a Pure Hitter

## Head and Hands

When a hitter is able to keep his head still it allows him to see the ball clearly and stay balanced. The swing should be finished with the head centered between both feet. Watch for whether the hitters head is staying still or moving. If the hitters head is moving up or down, it increases the possibility of a mechanical flaw in the swing. While this task of keeping your head still seems like a simple task it is not. The reason why it is so difficult is that the hitter wants to immediately see where the ball is traveling. However, what often happens is the head pulls away at the last second, and the hitter either fouls the ball away, or swings and misses. A key phrase that I use when coaching is, "See Contact." For the hitters with a bad habit of pulling their head away I have them not look at where the ball is traveling, rather just see contact and leave the head at that point of contact. I will often ask the hitter do you "feel" like you hit the ball well. Often that answer is yes, and they accomplished their goal of making contact.

Hitters need to learn how to take their hands to the ball as quick as possible in order to make contact on the barrel. However, I often see hitters taking the barrel to the ball first instead of the knob of the bat. For a hitter to have quick hands to the ball, pulling that knob to the inside half of the ball first while keeping it close to the chest is vital. The bottom hand pulls the knob, and the top hand takes the bat to contact.

This is called being "short to the ball." Remember, in the last chapter we discussed palm up and palm down at contact. The hands will be in this contact position, if the hitter has done the pulling of the knob the right way. Common traits of a player with slow hands are they are long to the ball, or in baseball terms they are "casting out." Instead of taking the knob of the bat to the inside part of the ball, they are taking the barrel to the outside part of the ball. When a player is "casting out" you will often see that contact occurs between the handle and barrel of the bat. When a hitter understands how to take their hands to the ball via the right and wrong way, they are on their way to becoming a consistent hitter.

## Balance and Legs

When a hitter is able to stay balanced it allows him or her to have a controlled swing. Balance starts with the stance. If the stance is not athletic, it increases the probability of poor balance. When looking at the stance check to see if the feet are wider than the shoulders, the knees are bent, and their weight is on their back foot. Now once the correct stance has been established the toughest task for hitters is to maintain balance during the swing. My favorite drill to check for balance is have the hitter hold their finish for two seconds and maintain the back-foot pivot. Now we as coaches are constantly telling kids to rotate or pivot their back foot. This is where we get into the lower half.

In order for a hitter to generate power and be balanced the hitter needs to understand how to use their lower body correctly. While we tell hitters to rotate their back foot don't forget about the back knee. The back knee needs to turn toward the front knee. To put a picture in your head, when thinking about the conclusion of the swing, the back leg will look like an L shape, and the front leg will be straight at around a 45-degree angle. The other aspect of the lower half to not neglect is the hips. When the swing is finished the hips need to be facing the pitcher. The hip turn is going to help start that torque to allow for the hands to snap to contact. Nevertheless, the back-foot pivot needs to still be addressed, especially to young hitters. Good phrases for young hitters to understand turning their back foot are: "Show the bubble gum on the bottom of your shoe to the catcher," "Show your shoelaces to the pitcher," "Squish the bug."

## Strike Zone and Count Hitting

The hitter needs to understand that the typical strike zone is the shape of a square horizontally from each corner of the plate and vertically from the hitter's knees to lower-point of the chest. The hitter must first understand where they are standing in relation to the plate. I often see kids take pitches down the middle of the plate because they thought it was either inside or outside. To measure the correct distance for the hitter to stand next to the plate, place the end of the bat on the corner of the outside part of the plate. The hitter will place his or her toes where the knob of the bat lies. This way you know the hitter can reach the outside corner of the plate.

Understanding what is a ball and what is a strike comes with repetition. Hitter's need to be disciplined enough not to swing at pitches outside the strike zone and be patient enough to wait for one that is in the strike zone. A great drill to work on is hitting balls from different heights in the strike zone from the inside, middle, and outside part of the plate from a tee. Make sure the hitter understands that not all umpires stay true to the strike zone and that the square might grow by more than an inch depending on who is umpiring. Despite the umpire's strike zone, the hitter should be aware of the correct size and work on only hitting balls in that strike zone.

The hitter's personal strike zone should decrease or expand depending on what the count is. Before the hitter steps into the box the hitter needs to understand that different counts can dictate what pitches the pitcher throws. Typically, when a pitcher is behind in the count you will see a fastball. When a pitcher is ahead in the count you will see an off-speed pitch. The three types of counts are:

**No Strike Count:** (0-0, 1-0, 2-0, 3-0) The hitter can be more selective and only swing at a pitch down the middle.

**One Strike Count:** (0-1, 1-1, 2-1, 3-1) The hitter has to be less selective and now should swing at pitches middle in and middle out.

**Two Strike Count:** (0-2, 1-2, 2-2, 3-2) The hitter has to expand their strike zone to the whole plate and swing at any pitch in or near the strike zone.

## Extension and Contact Points

Many young hitters have a tendency to pull away from the ball not allowing them to get extended. Explain to your hitter that you want him or her to swing "through" the baseball. When a player has grasped swinging through the ball it decreases the chances of him or her to roll the hands over before contact. A great phrase to say to a hitter is, "Pretend you are hitting through 3 baseballs instead of just 1." If you watch videos of Major League players, it is amazing at how much extension they get. You won't see a professional hitter finishing their swing low by their waist. If it is finishing low, the chances are good that he or she is not getting extended.

Getting extension through an inside, middle, and away pitch is something I don't see often talked about. It is important your hitter understands the swing doesn't change because the location of the pitch is different. The swing always stays the same, where contact is made is different. When contact is made the hitter has to get extension through that point in order to drive the ball. The inside pitch is the furthest point of contact out front of the plate, where the outside pitch is the nearest point. Nevertheless, understand that contact is always out front of the plate. I hear many coaches tell hitters, "You have to let the outside pitch get really deep." The problem by letting the ball get too deep is it is almost impossible to keep the ball fair. What us coaches have to get through to kids regarding the outside pitch is extension with the hands to the opposite field.

## Hitting for Power and Average

In order for a hitter to generate power the hitter needs to understand how to use their upper and lower body. Like I discussed earlier, the upper body involves a proper load, pulling of the knob inside the ball, and having palm up/palm down at contact. For the lower body remember 60 percent weight back, 40 percent forward, back foot rotated, and hips turned. Both the upper and lower body need to work together in order to generate power. With this being said, a common lack of power comes from a poor load, the body weight too far forward, not swinging hard, and only swinging with the upper body.

In order for your hitter to hit for more average the hitter needs to work on being consistent. Confidence, vision, balance, and a good mental and physical understanding of the mechanics of the swing increases the hitter's chances of making solid contact. Seeing the ball come out of the pitcher's hand, tracking the height and speed, all while swinging level is important to increasing the average. Hitters should never try to lift the ball in the air. Swinging up decreases the opportunity of making contact, which inherently lowers the average. Remember getting 3 hits out of 10 tries means you have a good batting average.

## Approach and Situational Hitting

All successful hitters have a mental game plan before they are at bat. Before the batter steps up to the plate he or she should have already had a simple offensive approach in mind. Learning to trust it makes it easier to respond to a pitch. The most consistent approach a hitter can have is to: "Think up the middle." Some examples other than up the middle thinking is: "Low line drive," "Level swing," "Hit it hard." Despite what their approach is, it should be simple and positive. As a hitter, ask yourself, "Are you defensively or offensively minded when hitting in a game?" The correct answer should be offensively minded because if you are defensively minded, you are not in control and are more worried than confident.

Now as your approach becomes consistent, you are more liable to execute an at bat in certain situations, which puts added pressure on the opposing team. There are certain situations in a game that call for these at bats. Sacrifice Bunting, Hit and Running, Runner on 2B with no one out, Runner on third base with less than two outs are typical hitting situations a hitter might be called upon to execute for the team.

**Sacrifice Bunting:** With a runner on 1B bunt the ball to the 1st base side, runner on 2B bunt the ball to the 3rd base side.

**Hit and Running:** No matter where the pitch is, the hitter must try to put the ball in play, preferably on the ground and out of the middle part of the field. The base runner will be stealing.

**Runner on 2B, no one out:** Look for a pitch on the right side of the plate so that you can hit the ball to the right side of the field. The goal is to get the runner to 3rd base or home.

**Runner on 3rd base, less than two outs:** Look for a pitch that is elevated to drive to the outfield. The goal is to score the runner on 3rd base.

# 16

# Coach Lopez

## Quotes for success

Confident individuals approach difficult tasks as challenges to be mastered rather than as threats to be avoided.

Failure is unavoidable.

Failure, after all, is the price we pay for success.

You must welcome the tough times and

view them as down payment for coming success.

Confidence is a choice.

Life reeks of mediocrity, are YOU a part of it?

Never let the opponent set the tempo.

Now is the time to become a MAN! You don't always attain EXCELLENCE, but you are DOOMED the day you stop seeking it!

INTENSITY AND EFFICIENCY

Question: How can you fail if you have these two traits?

Better Question: Do you have these traits?

Best Question: If you DON'T have these traits, WHY are you HERE?

The Greek word for "Race" is (Agon)

The very word from which we get our English word AGONY

A race is agonizing

10-80-10

Who are you? Your life will answer this question daily.

(**Authors Note**: 10-80-10 refers to lower 10 percent of people who are failures,

80 percent of people who are average, and the top 10 percent who seek excellence).

Can you take a punch?

I will PREPARE MYSLEF and be READY; Perhaps my chance will come!

This is a MAN!

Discipline, Poise, Intensity, Efficiency, Mental Toughness

Do you believe that these traits would lead you to success?

It's all about standards.

The goal is a tough road, you'll need shoes, don't show up bare foot.

I will die empty.

I will play hard every day.

Think about what YOU want to do, not what might happen to you.

The game honors toughness.

FEARLESS

Don't be afraid to make a physical mistake.